HOMESICK for HEAVEN

Books by Walter Starcke

THE DOUBLE THREAD
THE ULTIMATE REVOLUTION
THE GOSPEL OF RELATIVITY
HOMESICK FOR HEAVEN

HOMESICK for HEAVEN

You don't have to wait

Walter Starcke

GUADALUPE PRESS

Cover design by Bradford Lawton
Book design by Betsy Davis
Photography by Eron Howell

Library of Congress Cataloging-in-Publication Data
Starcke, Walter.
    Homesick for heaven: you don't have to wait/
Walter Starcke.
        p. cm.
    1. Mysticism—Miscellanea. 2. New Age move-
ment. I. Title.
BL625.S754   1988
291.4'2—dc 19   88-83304
ISBN 0-929845-04-8   CIP

FIRST EDITION

CONTENTS

PART II

The Experience

Introduction

I can't remember when I began to wonder if I hadn't gotten into this world by mistake. My appetite for life, even when quite young, included everything, excluded nothing. I wanted it all. I liked to do all the things that little boys like to do and I liked doing all the things that little girls like. I believed equally in the world I could touch and in fantasies I could dream. Impossibility seemed a commonly accepted lie.

Whenever I bumped up against arbitrary restrictions, I felt cheated out of the joy of life and required to fake myself. Religion, which inevitably appealed to me, perplexed me because I couldn't see why the love of God, of life, had to be inconsistent with the enjoyment of material pleasures. Sackcloth and ashes seemed unnecessary impositions.

In short, as imagination was stifled by conformity, I soon felt out of place or time. Heaven was my home and I was unable to see why I had to leave it in order to grow up. Even then I wanted to have my cake and eat it. I still do.

A lifetime of searching for a way back home has taken me around the world many times, to the feet of masters, and through a number of disciplines; it has given me at least a taste of all the luxurious pleasures that the world has to offer; most of all, it has ushered me into a number of almost totally different, sometimes glamorous but always successful professions. Finally, everything has come together. I no longer feel I am here by mistake. I am off the hook. The time is now. I am home again. This world is Heaven. I can, too, have my cake and eat it.

I know now that my problem wasn't in my trying to change the world into Heaven but rather in my finding the key that would turn the mental lock which had until now forbidden my entrance. At last I've found it. At least I feel I've closed the gap between my humanity and my divinity without having to reject either. I haven't had to get rid of my humanness, all its feelings and delights, and I haven't had to separate myself from the joys and freedoms of knowing God.

The world's collective consciousness has now reached a stage in its evolution, a shift which is now opening the gates of Heaven for all—not just for the so-called "spiritual" people, but for all. We are all homesick to be off the hook and back to the source. The steps I am going to offer here are the spiritual health aids I've swallowed in order to cure my sense of separation.

In a way, this is a spiritual autobiography. If I were to write a literal step-by-step account of my life involving all the famous names, my exotic visits to intriguing foreign secret places, the price I've paid for eating forbidden fruits, and all the rest, the book would be enormous and superficial. No, this is an autobiography only in that it paints a portrait of my spiritual journey in brief strokes of the pen. It's a map of my soul.

Believe me, I am not out to teach anyone anything. But I am out to share. I guess I want to share for a selfish reason. If I can lay my soul next to yours, we will be one, or rather I will better realize that we already are.

I want to share myself now because without doubt this extraordinary collective transitional experience that we are all going through is more dramatically changing our way of living than any social shift in the past. Because of the present breakthrough, all finite limitation is becoming obsolete and infinity is now available and achievable for all.

What's happening now is as significant for the expansion of the human mind and consciousness as Columbus's discovery of America was for geography. Until Columbus's voyage, humankind was limited by the belief that the world was flat, linear. After that geographical breakthrough, the world was found to be spherical, round, and self-contained. Until now, except for those few—those like Jesus, Buddha, Shankara, Echardt, Thielhard de Chardin—we have used our minds or awarenesses in a flat, linear fashion. For most of us, our consciousness radiates out, endlessly dissipating itself. Now we can be aware of the fact that we are multidimensional beings, and discover how we can live in a conscious simultaneity of time, space, and total beingness.

Like all of the most profound secrets, the answer was so simple, so right in front of my eyes, that I couldn't believe in its obvious importance when I first discovered it. I was in my early thirties when I stumbled onto the key and the past thirty-plus years have been involved with finding how to use it.

Nothing has been wasted; no mistake, or experience has been un-valuable. Everything I have gone through has been invaluably necessary in helping me to forge my own unique solution, a solution which has led me to the dominion and infinite freedom which we were all promised at the very beginning of our biblical parable. I have my message, my key to dominion, and this is it.

PART I

The Communication Complex

ONE

My Parable

After my typical Texas childhood, followed by college and duty as a Naval officer in the Second World War, I arrived in New York emotionally battered from several years of the military machine. I was swallowing things to pep me up and things to calm me down, but, to exercise a cliche, "ready to make my fame and fortune." This is not the time nor do I have the space to outline the soap opera aspects of my career or romantic adventures, except as they became the necessary counterpoints leading to my eventual discoveries. But I can say that even in those areas I left no stone unturned in my unconscious pursuit of experiencing everything.

After the regimentation and constriction of school and Navy life, I was automatically drawn to the freedom and fantasy of the theater world. Perhaps I subconsciously realized even then that the theater manipulated illusion and held a metaphysical answer for how to break this twenty-four-hour-a-day illusion.

Success came easily. With only a smattering of experience as an actor, I played three juvenile leads on Broadway my first year. But behind my bubbly smiling mask was a frightened and driven boy of twenty-four.

At any rate, I'm glad that the sophisticated artificial stimulants and drugs we have on the market today were not then the commonly accepted scene or I am sure I'd have explored that route in my attempt to leave no stone unturned. I tried drinking, but my stomach rebelled and the resultant hangovers were not worth it. I felt about as full of holes as a sieve and thought there were too many to be plugged up psychologically. Frantic, my search began not out of a desire to find a religion but from a very real necessity to simply cope. If I couldn't find a material pill to save me, I decided to gamble on finding a spiritual one that I could swallow.

It was at this point that I began my journey into the present. Without realizing it, I put my feet on two different spiritual paths. I won't jump the gun and explain the value of each at this point but I will say that one was the Eastern approach and the other the Western; one used the Oriental symbols and the other the Hebrew/Christian spiritual myth.

I quite consciously knew that a blanket, rote acceptance of my early orthodox Protestant upbringing alone wouldn't give the answers I was seeking. I thought that if I could study the world's religions, I might find truths which appeared in all of them and could therefore be accepted as true. I have never been very intellectual or good at detailed thinking, but I had a knack for skimmingly plucking out basic tenets without getting caught up in the mind-trapping fine print. Better still, I could slug my way through clumsy, complicated, and esoteric tomes, if there was something in them that resonated with my inner spirit.

The first Hindu based book I pulled off the shelf was *The Quest of the Overself* by Paul Brunton. In the late forties, the "find yourself" mania had not yet become a pop cliche but this book hinted that true identity was the key and it put the self into a divine perspective.

Coming from the "one way and only one way" proposition of orthodox Christianity which demanded conformity, I found Swami Vivikananda's series of yoga books a fantastic revelation. What appealed to me was that this was the first time I had discovered that I could experience God in my own way. I saw that the word "yoga" came from the Sanskrit meaning "union" or "path to union;" as there were many forms of yoga, so there were many ways I could arrive at union. I could get there according to my own unique bent and I didn't have to join anything to do it.

Little did I know then how, through pursuing Vivikananda's writings, I would soon become deeply involved with the Ramakrishna order and his once removed disciple, Swami Prabvananda.

As I was taking my first timid steps along the Eastern path, I was also setting out along the path of Western Christian mysticism. Through the first Broadway play in which I took part, I met the playwright, John van Druten, who was then New York's most outstanding author/director with his plays, *The Voice of the Turtle*, and *I Remember Mama*, both running to packed houses. Somehow we had gotten into a talk on spiritual matters and, sensing my hunger, he gave me some letters to read. They were letters from a Christian Science practitioner, Joel S. Goldsmith, who later went on to become one of the most significant metaphysical mystics of this age, teaching via the Christian symbols.

"From your Methodist background," van Druten said, "you probably won't understand these letters but read them and I will explain." Well, I must admit that coming from a family of doctors who roundly condemned Christian Scientists, I ferreted the writings home guiltily, though excitedly feeling as though I was about to take a look at some kind of spiritual pornography. Instead, the very first letter almost blew my head off. The "Yes, yes, yes" that exploded in me signaled an open door of enormous importance, even a life raft in a hopeless storm.

I'll admit that the language, though English, had a metaphysical ring that was foreign to me in contrast to the traditional theological pap to which I was accustomed. Picture the limited guilt-ridden, punishing God, the Hell and damnation religion to which I had been subjected and you will easily see why this first letter was like the hand of God reaching down to pluck me out of the sea of despair.

> Dear Friend:
> Jesus said: "Ye are the light of the world." Do you believe this? If you are the light, is there any darkness in you at all? If you are the light, can any light be added to you? Are you not the light—full and complete and bright? "I am the light of the world"—and ever will be— and if you accept this teaching you will shine as the noonday sun in which there is no darkness at all. "I am the light" will not permit questions of why or wherefore. It accepts itself as the full radiance of the risen sun. "I am the light" seeks not for light, health, wealth, success, progress, but knows "I am." That which I am seeking, I am.
> Jesus never said: "I will be resurrected" but he did say "I am the resurrection"—I am the power itself. He never spoke of seeking the Truth, using Truth, applying Truth, but he said: "I am the Truth." And remember he not only said, "I am the light" but also "Ye are the light of the world." "Greater works shall ye do." Is all this true? Do you accept the truth that "I am the truth"? When you abide steadfastly in this consciousness, all the petty trials and the big problems of human existence fade away because "to truth there is no error"—to "life there is no death."

Sing within yourself, morning, noon and night, "I am the life, the truth, the light." Let a song of joy and grateful recognition surge through your being and know that the divine being is your only being. This being is all-inclusive life, love, substance, law and reality. You do not any more get "at one with truth" or seek some truth with which to meet a need, but you realize with infinite joy, "I am the truth."

"Ye are the light of the world." As you rest in this consciousness, you will no longer find it necessary to "overcome evil"—"destroy error"—"battle mortal mind." As the light, darkness vanishes as you approach it and you have no consciousness of the darkness that has been dispelled, not any more than intelligence can be aware of the ignorance it displaces.

This "I Am" is the universal Being, your Christ-Self, your true identity, the only one you have.

With kind regards, I am,

Sincerely yours,
Joel S. Goldsmith

Talk about "Let a song of joy and grateful recognition surge through your being" . . . sing I did and the surge became a tidal wave. Bells rang in my spirit. It wasn't just the words. I don't think I really understood them anyway, but the spirit, the vibration, the tone of the letter resonated deeply within me. It was Heaven announcing itself. It let me know there was a way, a source, a call. I knew then that spiritual homesickness could be cured.

When I saw van Druten the next day, instead of his explaining the letter to me, I rattled with youthful know-it-all-ness that this was what I had always instinctively felt but had not seen in words before. My hunger for more was unabated.

Thus this two-pronged journey through Oriental and Christian mysticism began, a journey which took seven years to lead me to the beginning of the real purpose and message of my own life.

The Approach

It was happening. For the next seven years I did indeed find truths that reappear in all the major revelations. As it turned out, however, it wasn't the obvious similarities which uncovered the secret but rather the differences—not so much the differences in ideas as where emphasis was placed differently. All roads may lead to Rome but the road signs may send us endlessly chasing our own tails unless we understand and appreciate the uniqueness of each approach and discover some universal sign language which can eliminate the duality by integrating the individual contribution of each. What each approach revealed about the other was perhaps even more important than what it showed about itself.

I was constantly faced with the paradox of duality, if not multiplicity. While my more dominant social, sexual, and professional life was centered around New York, my sorties into the spiritual dimension sent me to California, as both the Swami Prabvananda's Vedanta Society and Goldsmith's home were there.

I'll never forget my first visit to the Vedanta monastery. It shook me to the core. The Society had and still has a remarkable convent in lush Santa Barbara with a temple that is one of the most authentic representations of ancient Oriental architecture in this country. In Hollywood, they have a quiet and pleasant complex where Christopher Isherwood, Aldous Huxley, Gerald Heard, and other intellectuals of that period would often be found attending services. But the monastery high in the hills above Laguna Beach, off charming eucalyptus-filled Trabuco Canyon, holds a most special place in my life.

The monastery is comprised of a compound of graceful Spanish style buildings of red brick and white plaster with arched tile-roofed arcades surrounding flower bedecked patios. The main lodge includes the monks cells, dining room, kitchen, library, and the lounge with its welcoming fireplace where guests and monks would gather around Swami after dinner. Dressed in a soft pastel cashmere sweater and graceful linen slacks, he would perch in a comfortable overstuffed chair, most often tucking his feet under him, and gently, lovingly, discourse on ancient Vedas to a most appreciative assembly. The love in his beautiful face would have thawed a deep freeze.

Next to the main building, connected by a passage, is the sanctuary, a unique, round, windowless building. At the entrance, there is a small shoe room, a room where shoes are left before approaching the inner sanctum. Entering, it takes a moment for the eyes to adjust to the sole illumination of the candle twinkling altar with its shiny vessels, bowls of fruit, scattering of flowers, and soul wrenching picture of Ramakrishna reaching out with eyes personally calling you to another world.

Every day, there is a community meditation for an hour before breakfast, again before lunch, and before dinner. From the moment I entered the shrine, it was as though I was breathing air for the first time in my life. Despite the discomfort of sitting in the unfamiliar cross-legged position for hours at a time, they had to practically drag me from the temple at the end of each meditation so life-time starved was I for the experience. I can easily say that the single most valued gift to life that I received from the Vedanta Society was meditation.

This was the first time in my life that I had been in an ambience of spirit where a group of active lively men met each other with such unthreatening open honesty, clear-eyed love, and understanding compassion.

I saw people in a spiritual context whose words and actions matched. The Swami's unrestricted, unconditional acceptance washed all guilt away. I felt I was not only breathing air for the first time, but walking on it as well.

Though I was there for only a few days on this initial visit, by the time I had made the hour and a half drive back into Hollywood, my head was splitting from reentry shock, by nightfall the effect of returning to the dog-eat-dog world was so disturbing that I was vomiting. Part of me wanted to return and never to leave, and yet part of me knew that was not to be.

Goldsmith

Simultaneously with and in total contrast to my initial visit to the monastery was my first experience of Joel Goldsmith. Two things had happened which made it mandatory that I eventually meet Joel in person. First, I had been introduced to him through the letters van Druten had given me. Second, later that year I had worked with the grand old actress, Dame Mae Whitte, who was also a student of Joel's and she had talked constantly of him with awe.

At the end of a summer tour with Dame Mae, I hopped on a plane and made my first West Coast trip to see Joel. Van Druten met me at the airport and took me to his apartment. He told me that Goldsmith had written his first book, *The Infinite Way*, and that he, John, was writing the introduction. I actually read it before Joel did and the reading added to my sense of destiny as I anticipated my first meeting with this mysterious and impressive healer.

I remember the day I arrived at Joel's office as vividly as I remember the monastic experience with Swami Prabvananda but for totally different reasons. I arrived at a typical professional office building on bustling, auto-honking, smog-generating, Hollywood Boulevard, went up the elevator to the door of a sterile business office and knocked for entrance, again hoping that my deceased physician ancestors were not turning over in their graves as they watched me about to enter a door with a sign saying "Christian Science." As I waited there, I expected to be awed by this spiritual giant, this fatherly, benevolent master. The door opened and there before me was a five foot four, smiling, round, curly-haired, pink little Jewish man in a plaid sport coat and a flowered shirt; who looked more like someone who should be at a race track than at a place where one goes to be spiritually healed. And, what's more, the guy spoke with a New York accent.

When I finally stopped trying to impress Joel and began to listen to him, I felt a totally different kind of inner feeling than I had had at the Hindu temple. The bare functional office didn't exalt my esthetic emotions and Joel didn't make me want to sit at his feet and be warmed by his personality, but there was something behind his words that made me feel as though I was someone else whom I had never known, someone I would love to be. I felt power. Here was a force I wanted to possess. Here was freedom. Perhaps because of his Jewish background, his passion for freedom illuminated his words and, what's more, he spoke in the language of the Scripture of my childhood. Familiar quotes of Jesus sounded totally new. Joel spoke with an authority of presence as one who had been there.

Freedom means power and something in this man was power-full. I felt he not only knew where Heaven was, and how to get there, but also how to protect it.

Though there were many similarities between these two mystical paths, the Oriental and the Occidental, both eventually gave me a new perspective on the Christian message. By studying the Hindu path, I was able to turn around and see or understand Jesus's life and words free from the brain washing interpretation of traditional theology. I could honestly see Jesus as an avatar, a special revelator, a giant among other giants. I later learned what was unique about his life because I was able to see what was unique in the life of each of the great teachers. I was blessed in being able to wash off previous images and see for myself.

I also grew to realize that I wasn't born into the culture and symbols of my background by accident. None of us are. I needed to travel the world in order to gain perspective, knowledge, and experience but in the end I knew I had to reconcile my findings with the symbols of my youth in order to be truly free. I didn't need to agree with them, but to understand them.

Swami had given me an Oriental, less restricted, and more comprehensive approach to life than the narrow and logical Protestant one of my background, but most of all he gave me meditation. I had, indeed, discovered and developed helpful techniques, and had cultivated an appetite for meditation from my Vedanta association. Meditation then became central to my life, but an experience I had with Joel years later turned my life into a meditation.

I guess I need to tell you the story of the moment my experiential fire was lit through a meditation encounter I had with Joel which led to my breakthrough in Hawaii, when I discovered the purpose of my life.

During these early years, my later twenties, I continued as an actor except for a brief stint as a television director for Paramount Pictures in Hollywood where I had gone to study with both Joel and the Vedantists. Returning to New York from this sojourn, I charged ahead, determined to live by my newly found spiritual beliefs.

Each morning I would set aside some time to read from both the Hindu scriptures and Goldsmith's metaphysics and to perform what I thought was meditation. I was more centered, more under control and no longer felt the need for either stimulants or tranquilizers. Incidentally, in order to be free to write his own book, Goldsmith had left the Christian Science establishment.

So each morning I would read, meditate, and then go about my daily pursuit of work. This habit, or need if you will, was already changing my life; in order to make space for it each morning, I had to get to bed earlier than the A.M. bedtimes of my theater friends. Before long I wasn't part of the pack anymore.

At any rate, I charged out firm in faith, up in spirit, anchored in meditation. But, alas, after my return to New York, only bits and pieces of work came about and my bank account, the other side of the spiritual coin, went down and down. Finally I wrote Joel to ask him what was going on and got back a letter asking me, "Who do you think you are? Why don't you go out and work for a living?" I answered, "You said that if there was one theater in the world and I had the consciousness of theater I would be at work in it." I got back a worse letter. So I said, "Well, he is just an instrument through which God speaks. He doesn't even understand his own message. I'll go on reading his books but I won't have anything to do with him anymore."

I went out the very next day and won the most important part I had ever had as an actor. I got the juvenile lead in a play called *Detective Story*, which went on to win all kinds of honors, where I was on the stage all but seven minutes of the play.

Perhaps that is because I was no longer looking for Joel to be a witch doctor and was turning to something within myself; nevertheless the play opened in, of all places, Detroit. It opened on the one and only week that Goldsmith had ever been in Detroit in his spiritual career. So, as Joel didn't know I wasn't going to talk to him again, I called him on the phone. He invited me to come over to his hotel for a visit.

For the first time in our association, I came right out and questioned him. I remember I said, "If you tell me that sin, sickness, poverty, and such have no power at some spiritual level, I can understand that, but to me as a human being, they are a power." He answered, "Precisely. And if you want to stay a human being under those laws, help yourself, but you don't have to." Bang, I'd never realized what choice meant or could do.

Then, for the first time in our association, he said, "Let's meditate." I sat on one side of the room, he on the other. He put his brown Bible on his lap and we began. After a few minutes, I felt a complete shock go through my body from my tail bone up to the top of my head. One could say it was the opening of the kundalini—the seven centers that Hindus believe start at the base of the spine and end at the top of one's head. At any rate, I dismissed it at the time as unimportant. We finished, and I went back to my own hotel. Once again I sat to meditate; the same thing happened and I realized the experience wasn't accidental.

Having once experienced it, maintaining, sustaining, and repeating that contact in meditation became my whole life. I'd been satisfied with my meditations before that time. They helped me focus my life and be more productive, but this was different. This was like being exploded into Heaven.

It took a long time before I realized how totally my life had been affected by making this inner contact. Anything that interrupted it had to go. I didn't give up any of the so-called physical pleasures for moral reasons but one by one I did eliminate them if I felt they had a hold on me or in any way decreased the availabilty of making this contact. If anything interrupted or made meditation more difficult, out. Perhaps all of this was necessary in order to make it possible for me to have the experience I eventually had at Haleakala crater in Hawaii on the island of Maui.

The Secret

The breakthrough took place when I was thirty-two, several years after my meditation experience. By this time, my spiritual search had moved me out of being an actor and into producing plays.

When I co-produced *I Am a Camera,* from which the musical *Cabaret* was later made, at thirty-one, I was then the youngest producer on Broadway to have won the New York Drama Critics Circle Award. In more ways than one, my success was the outcome of my search up to that point. On one hand, the play was the story of Christopher Isherwood whom I had come to know through the Vedanta monastery and it was written and directed by van Druten, who also shared my associations with both Vedanta and Goldsmith. On the other hand, the metaphysical principles I had learned certainly contributed to closing the gap between the spiritual world and the marketplace. Whenever I followed the inner guidance I received through meditation, it was infallible. I even felt guilty for taking credit for my successes, as they came about simply because I followed inner orders.

Nevertheless, at this point, something still seemed to be missing from each of the two approaches to the spiritual life I was following. When I was at the monastery, I loved the way people related to each other, their thoughtful consideration, their warmth and the joy of meditation, but there was also a constant put down of material things. Sex was a no-no, money was poison, denial was the name of the game. I couldn't help but believe even then that if God had created all, it must all be good. I knew that absolutely anything could be used for evil if it were in its wrong place, not doing what it was created for. At the same time, the laws of condemnation which people invented in order to eliminate misuse seemed to create the very thing they were meant to eliminate.

When I returned from the monastery to New York, I was comfortably surrounded by people who didn't reject sex or money—quite the opposite. I felt at ease with their lack of man-made moral judgments but along with their enjoyments, they didn't leave space for or tune in to each other's souls, didn't experience their inner being through meditation. Their treasures were all external. I felt they missed something because they were not aware of their delicious divinity.

On the other hand, the Christian-based metaphysicians I encountered on retreats, and in seminars or metaphysical classes were often cold and unfeeling. Through their spiritual studies, they seemed to have achieved dominion over materiality but they remained disdainful toward other human beings and their problems. They rejected overt human affection. Compassion was in short supply. Everywhere, East or West, I still felt out of place.

In the summer of 1952, I went to see Joel in Hawaii for an extended period intending then to go to the monastery in California for a visit. One day Joel took me over to the island of Maui for a few days. The Baldwins, who were the dominant family on the island, were students of Joel's and he also wanted to introduce me to a couple of Hawaiian Kahuna friends. The Baldwins lent me a car with which to explore the island while Joel was having appointments; so I took off.

The first drive I took was up to the top of Haleakala to catch a glimpse of the fabled human-size silver sword flowers which share their majesty with us only there in the moonscape crater. The giant crater, where Hawaiians believe the sun was born, is a giant bowl with a twenty mile circumference. I arrived at the observation house 10,800 feet above the ocean and found that the crater was filled with clouds; the famous flowers growing in the crater weren't to be seen. Fooled by the fact that it was T-shirts and short pants warm at the beach, I found it was sweater frigid up there. In order to get out of the cold, I ignored the "Don't get off the path" sign and crawled around the edge of the rim until I found a hollow in the lava rock, a small, protective body-size cave. I nestled in, watched the mists spill over the crater edge like a boiling witch's caldron, and waited for the clouds to leave.

In no particular hurry, I drifted into meditation. For the first time in my life, with such "other world" clarity, I began to hear a kind of tape recording in my head. There wasn't any booming lordly voice but rather a quality of soul gently asking me questions.

Love

The subject was love. I don't remember the exact words at this point but the meanings were indelible. It asked, "What is love? You say you'd love an ice cream cone. Is that what love is? You say you'd just love to go to Paris. Is that what love is?" Immediately I thought of my two teachers, Swami and Joel.

As I have implied, Swami was everything the artistic and sensitive side of my being responded to. His surroundings were always the epitome of taste and gentle pastel beauty. There were always flowers, always lovely works of art, always exquisite tastes and smells, always quiet and gentle people around who made me feel joyously welcome. His aristocratic bearing, personal beauty and irresistible smile never failed to warm me. Here was material presence at its most artistic and soul satisfying.

When I came into Swami's presence, tears of welcome would come into his eyes. I felt special and loved. If I had a stomach ache and told him of it, his concern melted me with love. He cared. In fact, he was so concerned that I didn't mind having the stomach ache. But when I left him, however, I still had the stomach ache. I didn't care but I still had it.

Then I thought of Joel. He was a pleasant enough, ordinarily unnoticeable, puckish little man. Nothing in the material world meant much to him. His home, when he was wifeless and on his own, was functional and no more. His tastes were simple, basic, and uninspired. We had little to talk about outside of spiritual matters because my appetite for the good life had no appeal or interest for him. He abhorred extravagance and poverty equally. His paradise existed in an invisible world.

When I came into Joel's presence, he smiled welcomingly but somehow I felt he was as happy to see me go as to come. He treated few people specially and those were the ones who particularly helped him in his passion to get his message out. But, and it's a big "but," you could roll on the floor in front of Joel in pain and after a while he would frown, snap his fingers and say, "Get up, get up," and you'd get up healed. "Well," I thought, sitting on the edge of the crater, "if both of those are love, which do I want?"

Remember, I was hearing all of this, hearing it at a level of honesty I had not experienced before. My innate desire to have it all flashed before me and I said out loud, "I want both." I realized then that I am a man of earth who needs to be touched, loved, held, exercised, fed, clothed, and amused. I am also a man of God who must not be limited by this human body cage, who must fly, who must heal, who must be transcendent.

I realized then that Swami had the secrets of the good human life, the good earthly life, the way human beings could live lovingly together, and that Joel had the answer to true identity, to eternality, to freedom from the limitations imposed in finite being, to the mystical life.

Then it happened—returning to the thought of love itself, I realized that the secret, the vital, all-important, and unseen secret of the New Testament was that Jesus gave us *two* love commandments, not just one. He gave us the Christian paradox, an apparent duality, a double approach, as the way to find true oneness. He said to love God and to love neighbor, both. In saying, "Love God and add to it another commandment which is like unto the first," he was saying that they were not the same. They were alike but not the same. He was also saying we should take the first commandment and implied we should throw the other nine away—at least that we don't need the other nine if we lump them together and create a new commandment, love our neighbor.

In simple terms, I saw that these two commandments told us that we should love both *cause* and love *effects*. Cause is impersonal, invisible, and the source of all being, but effect is anything that has been personalized, anything that you can name, define, touch, smell, or conceptualize. Indeed, the two are like each other because, as the song says, "you can't have one without the other." Loving one without loving the other is not only impossible but, if there is too much concentration on one, it makes loving the other impossible. These two are like each other but they are not the same. You have to see each one in its own terms in order to reconcile them.

I saw or heard too, that all the religions of the world had fallen into a trap. They had all set as their mutual goal the revelation of an all-present, all-knowing, all-powerful God or spiritual presence but, on the way, due to emphasis rather than difference, by not knowing what it meant to love both the cause and the effect, they had created the very duality they were trying to eliminate. Wanting to love God, they had rejected materialty. They talked about equality without practicing it and sin was the result. Humanity was inevitably rejected because the love of God was not understood, and God was misunderstood because people tried to make Him human.

I don't want to get too far ahead of myself at this point because the rest of this book reveals the conclusions I arrived at as the result of over thirty years exploring my discovery of just how we can close the gap between our God self and our neighbor self. From that moment on, everything I saw or thought translated itself into one or the other of these two commandments.

To continue with the rest of the inner mystical tape recording I was hearing that morning, my next thought was, "Then how does Joel's form of love heal people?" Right away the Scripture, "Know ye no man after the flesh," popped into my head. Jesus's capacity to heal was embodied in His refusal to accept the appearance or the personality as the reality of a person; rather He experienced the divine eternal spiritual nature of the person and that's what healed them. Healing wasn't a matter of thought, but of experience. The capacity not to judge by appearances represented the commandment to love our neighbor.

The next thought was, "Then if the way I love effects is by not judging them materially, how do I love God?" Before I could hear anything, the sun broke out in all its glory. My little cave became a luminous shrine and spread before me was such a glamorous spectacle as you can't believe. The mists lifted and miles of multicolored mystical grandeur danced before my eyes. The fabled human-size silver sword flowers dotted the crater like sun sentinels announcing that God does appear in the visible world.

The Needle

What I thought had been minutes had transcended the time continuum by hours and I descended from the crater to join others for lunch. I was hesitant to leave because I knew the full message wasn't completed yet, so I sort of pushed down an internal "pause" button and left. What a day! At lunch, when I was once more at sea level, someone told me that I should go up Ioa Valley and take a look at the "Needle." I felt the inner "Yes," so in the afternoon I headed that way.

The "Needle" is a monolithic twenty-story tower of volcanic rock magically centered in a lush green valley floored by a rushing stream fed by a mysterious rain forest. It is only a short drive up the valley and a short walk to observation spots. In those days, it wasn't the tourist haven it has become, so I was all alone when I arrived.

The drive is only a couple of miles up the valley, but the curious thing is that though the sun is blazing away below as you turn the final approach, it is usually blotted out by mists and hovering clouds. On that particular day, I sat shivering in the dank chill trying fruitlessly to meditate. Finally I heard, "It's hard to believe that the sun is shining so intensely just around that corner, isn't it?" And then I realized an important key to the love of God, which had been left out earlier in the day. It said, "Walter, the same sun which broke out in all its glory at the crater is still shining around the corner." And I realized that to me, as a human being sitting in the dank grey mist, the sun seemed to have died. In fact the sun had produced the very clouds which hid it. What's more, the sun did it for my own good. The clouds brought the rain and the rain made the lush flower garden valley possible. I saw then that the way I could love God was to realize that despite appearances God is the only power. Well, actually the only cause.

I suspect you know what happened. As soon as that realization broke through into my consciousness, the sun once more broke through and the valley glistened in the sparkling shiny wetness.

With the arrival of the two aspects of this two-commandment message, the most important single day of my life was complete. I also had my passport to Heaven. Now I had to learn how to use it.

TWO

The Double Thread

When I came down from the mountain top, so to speak, I knew I had my work cut out for me. What had been revealed to me as the secret of the New Testament was telling me to love both my spiritual being and my human one. If I wasn't man of earth or man of God but both, my problem was not trying to eliminate either but getting those two aspects of myself to communicate with each other and to work together.

As I got deeper and deeper into the two-commandment message, my life began to sort itself out at every level and a kind of rhythm or harmony began to manifest itself. Even my health changed. I had always had a sinus problem, had been a bit too thin, and had been bothered by a trick stomach. All of that went away, not through miraculous healing, but through a change in consciousness that introduced a unity of body, mind, and spirit. I had a long way to go, but it was a beginning.

I started to separate and work with my spiritual and human selves, each on its own terms, knowing that if I succeeded, they would be "like unto each other" at the end.

New York became my monastery, my uniquely two-commandment monastery. The city, which both fascinated and appalled me, was the place where I had to meet life head on. If I could be at peace and experience God there, where humanity was at its most intensive, then I knew I could do it anywhere and communicate with all of life.

As my life improved, friends who saw my progress wanted to know what was happening and began pulling answers out of me; so, some fourteen years after the Maui experience, I wrote a book. I was pushed into it. I hadn't made particularly good grades on my themes in school and the last thing I wanted to do was to get involved in either the author racket or the spiritual one, but there wasn't a single book to which I could refer my friends where the double concept was clearly communicated or emphasized; so I decided to make a stab at it.

At first I didn't take the writing business too seriously, and I wrote the first draft in ten days. I intended to pay for a few copies out of my own pocket through a vanity press just to give to friends, but I let several people read the manuscript in its initial form and they all said, "Someone will publish this;" so I thought I might as well start at the top and sent it to Harper & Row.

As proof that the spirit works in miraculous ways, Harper's religious department needed an off-beat metaphysical book in a big hurry at precisely that moment. A week after the manuscript landed on his desk, the editor called to ask if I would work on it for quick publication. I was amazed and delighted.

When the subject of the title came up, my editor expressed what seems to be a publisher's syndrome, if not prerogative; he wanted me to change the title I had put on the manuscript. He felt it didn't zero in on what the book was really about. He was right. In fact, he wanted a new title by Monday because the catalog needed to go to press. Well, I thought and thought and couldn't come up with anything. In desperation, I decided to stop worrying and to still my mind by continuing to read a book I had recently begun by Pierre Teilhard de Chardin, *The Divine Milieu.* In the book, there was a prayer which in substance was Teilhard de Chardin's recognition of the neccessity of the double thread. It said, "Lay hold on me fully, both by the Without and the Within of myself. Grant that I may never break this double thread of my life." The words "double thread" leaped out at me; I had my title: *This Double Thread.*

The point is that more than fourteen years after I discovered Jesus's "double thread" secret, I hadn't yet realized the full scope of his instruction. I was still seeing what had happened to me on Maui only as a rather personal and simple revelation designed just to help me balance myself. When I mentioned it to other people, I mainly emphasized that things were not either/or. I explained that they were not either men of earth *or* men of God. They were both, and that the two were not the same. I would repeat, "Your man of earth self needs to be fed, exercised, clothed, kept clean, and, above all, loved, touched, caressed, and welcomed. Your man of God self has to be freed from his human cage and be allowed to fly. Your man of earth self has limits but your man of God self must communicate with infinity."

When the book actually came out in print, I had second thoughts about it. It seemed so naïvely obvious. I thought the fact that nothing was either/or, was so fundamental that it didn't really need to be stated, but at that point I hadn't realized how few were able to think without excluding one side or the other, nor how few could see the exquisite ramifications of the principle, how really far reaching it was. I hadn't yet seen how communicating these two commandments affects every aspect of life, even how the future and survival of the world now depend on it.

Now, twenty-one years since that first publication, I often get letters from people who write that they appreciated *This Double Thread* when it came out, but that lately something has made them take it off the shelf and in rereading they were blown away by its relevance for today. They say how it has helped them communicate with their whole beings at a time when communications affect every aspect of life.

The Importance of Communications

The day of the supernatural is over. Twentieth century science has unveiled and demystified the unknown and occult. This more profound knowledge of the workings of the brain and public acceptance of humankind's inherent intuitive faculty has taken what was in the past considered to be supernatural or miraculous and has revealed it to be simply the "supra-natural." We no longer have to superstitiously believe extra-phenomenal happenings but can discern and reveal the principles behind psychic, spiritual, and supra-natural experience in ways we were unable to before.

With the advent of the communications explosion, secrets that were the exclusive domain of the shamans, magicians, and witch doctors have now become public property. Hitler was one of the first to deliberately take over, and exploit these heretofore secret powers through the use of modern communication techniques. In America, Roosevelt captured the mind of the country via the communications media. Madison Avenue jumped on the band wagon and has employed and often misused powerful witch doctor techniques to manipulate millions. Those secrets are out in the open now, so we had better expose them and explain how these powers can be controlled and used for the betterment of all mankind or we will truly end life on earth as we know it.

The forces of darkness—mental, physical, or spiritual—know that the way you imprison an individual or a nation is through the mind, through communications and the effect on the imaginations and, therefore, the spirits of the people. Charlatans also know that the best way to hide a secret is to put it right out in front of everyone and make it so obvious that they miss it.

The techniques which can imprison mankind are the same ones we can use to heal and uplift it. Anything that can free us can also imprison us—and vice versa. All manipulation techniques relate to communications, the use of false or true identity, confusion or clarity, separation or union. Through communication, we divide and conquer or unite and survive.

As I became aware of these techniques, I realized the witch doctor's secret. They didn't do anything. They just dangled the carrots of fear, ignorance, false identity, and desire; stimulated by desire, the images that people had allowed into their consciousnesses imprisoned them. I found that no one had ever imprisoned me. I had always done it to myself.

I realized that if I wanted to be free and stay that way, I would have to communicate with a more profound sense of my own identity, with others, and with a greater understanding of the outside world. That's what loving God and neighbor was all about. It would take clarity. It would take purity. It would take practice. And it would take honesty.

Honesty is not a matter of desire. It is a matter of capacity. Most of us want to be honest, but as long as we are brainwashed, as long as we don't have a clear picture of who we are, and until we can communicate, we don't have the capacity to be honest even if we desire to be. If we can't be honest, we can't communicate with ourselves or anyone.

I am writing this book now, twenty-one years after my first, because there has been a breakthrough now in the collective consciousness which makes communications possible to a greater depth, among a greater number of people, and to a greater extent than ever before. Some have called it "the harmonic convergence." No matter what it is called, what has made us aware of the need to unite the flesh and the spirit is also making a collective realization available to all. I am sharing my example to show how I learned to communicate with God, myself, and then with others.

Cluster Communication

A body is just a body until it moves. When it moves, its movement communicates something. You are what you communicate. You are a "double thread," both a body and what it communicates and each communication has a spiritual quality.

It's no accident that the "new age" is also called "the communications age." Communication is another of those matters that we must now see in terms of "cluster" rather than the one-dimensional "linear" interpretation that we have limited ourselves with in the past. Our bodies communicate, our minds communicate, our spirit communicates and each of these levels also has different simultaneous nuances. Communication is not only a cluster-like multi-dimensional experience; it is most importantly a spiritual matter. Every communication has a spirit content and conveys a spiritual message.

Before my Maui experience, the Bible had been a closed book for me but when I was able to see what love meant in a new way, it began to communicate with me or I with it. To my surprise, I found that the New Testament is really a communications manual. Once Jesus had caught his vision of spiritual reality, he dedicated his life to defining and communicating it. His every word was an attempt to explain the importance of communicating truth and righteous judgment, and to give instructions for how we could communicate with each other, with ourselves, and ultimately with God. What good is there in knowing of a divine presence if we can't communicate with it?

After all, "In the beginning was the Word" (communication), and the Word was made flesh. The Word is also spirit. Everything is spirit-formed, spirit-communicating. When we stop thinking in linear terms, we see, as Teilhard de Chardin told us, that everything, no matter how dense, has consciousness, communicates something. Mundane objects such as tables and chairs communicate. Put a board across two stumps and we call it a table because it communicates a function. There are no nouns anyway, only verbs connoting functions. Everything we see is a symbol of that which created it and a symbol of the spirit it represents.

It is important to relate our spiritual life to communications because we are all little broadcasting stations. Every thought we conceive and every act we perform communicate our spirit and create our world. When we can stand aside and see how our universe is sending out a spiritual message, we can communicate with reality. A doctor is supposed to be in the business of communicating health. A plumber communicates plumbing, a teacher knowledge. As such, there isn't a single problem that doesn't come about except for a miscommunication or a lack of communication. Ignorance is simply miscommunication.

I'm laboring the idea of communications because, if we can define terms, reveal extended cluster levels of personal and divine reality, we can, through communication, experience God and each other. Communication has suprising ramifications.

The Double Thread of Communications

I began to communicate with myself when I realized that the way we are tricked out of communicating is by accepting the harmful belief that absolutes are possible at this finite level. Absolutes do exist but not at the less-than-absolute level of phenomena, of multiplicity. Humanly, there are no two of anything alike.

I might manufacture a million water glasses, each of which looks exactly alike to the naked eye, but under a microscope each one is a bit different. Which one is the perfect one? And if I choose one as perfect then I condemn all the others. As human beings, it is impossible to be absolute, the finite can't be infinite. By thinking we can or should be absolute, we can't help but feel guilty. Absolutes are abstractions and humans are not abstract. Our Christ may be absolute but our humanity is not.

The question isn't whether we are finite or infinite, perfect or imperfect, mortal or immortal, but whether we identify ourselves with the limitation and body or with infinity and freedom. We are not dealing with a dualistic universe, but with one and the same reality, seen from two different dimensions: the personal neighbor side or the impersonal infinite and ego-free spirit.

Again, our problem is not "either/or" but "as-well-as"; we are the center between Heaven and Earth, the place where Heaven and Earth meet, not absolutely either without the other. In other words, it is the finite that gives meaning to the infinite, because the infinite appears as the finite. By the same token, East and West are two halves of our human consciousness, like the two poles of a magnet, which can't be separated into absolute differences. Only when we realize this fact, will we become complete human beings able to communicate wholly or "Holy-ly."

The danger in the West stems from our overemphasis on the worldly pole of absolute individuality, of egocentric motivation, of self-assertiveness, and a dominance of will power. In the East, the danger lies in the overemphasis of the absolute universal pole, the spiritual, the metaphysical, the negation of the value of individuality, which leads to a formless unity. Both approaches contradict the law of spiritual existence: one denies universality, the other deprives the individual of his or her value. An overemphasis on unity can be as great a mistake as the overemphasis on plurality.

I used to demand absolutes or perfection of myself and carried around the biggest bag of guilt possible. Finally I realized that, if I wanted to be a perfect living human, I had to have flaws and opposites. They keep me growing.

In every creative act, there is something that could be called destructive. If I want to build a house, I have to cut the trees down. Whenever we create any new thing, the old form has to be destroyed in order for the new to take its place. At the human level, perfection is relative to the process. At the absolute level where human nature does not exist, abstract perfection exists but it is inactive perfection. At the level where all individuality creatively expresses itself, there is no frozen single standard.

I remember once I went to Joel Goldsmith with a hang up that I had. Instead of advising me to discontinue my "sin," he said, "Just make your contact with God (communicate) and, when your problem has served its purpose, it will go away." So I became an idealist rather than a perfectionist or absolutist. The difference is that absolutists have to feel guilty when they aren't perfect whereas idealists can aim at perfection, fail, pick themselves up, and try again without depriving themselves of self-love.

The ideal is neccessary. We go much further by aiming at perfection but not if we sacrifice the love of our self in exchange for absolutes which deny infinite individual being.

Psychology and Mysticism

During my absolutist period, the period when I was most lonely, I looked down on my friends who were going to psychologists and psychiatrists for help. I thought that everything should be handled purely spiritually. Later I realized that psychology and mysticism are two different methods of communication and I had been excluding one. Having experienced a degree of my divinity, I knew that the difference between the approach of a mystic and that of a psychologist were one hundred eighty degrees in opposition but not necessarily in conflict. I had mistakenly judged psychology without holistically communicating myself.

In order to fully communicate the "double thread," it is important to know the difference between the psychological and the mystical. The psychological involves the intellect and learning, the mystical involves intuition and spirit. The intellect is a necessary tool for overcoming emotionality and spiritual confusion. Intuition is necessary for overcoming stagnant concepts and intellectual limitation. The intellect outlines a path but without intuition the experience of God is impossible. Lama Govinda once wrote:

> Those who live only in their emotions are like a rudderless ship; the merely intellectual—but aimless—individual is like a ship without a driving force, whose rudder does not find the necessary resistance to act upon and, there-

fore, exhausts itself in useless movements without any effect. Applied to the human condition, this results in empty activities and spiritual stagnation. On the other hand, a man whose intellect stops halfway, incapable of pursuing a subject or problem to its last possible conclusion, or who regards the problem only in a partial or one-sided way, is like a helmsman who moves the steering-wheel in only one direction and whose ship, therefore, runs in circles.

The solution to this condition isn't to reject the intellectual or psychological approach but to use it in a more enlightened and fuller manner directed toward the mystical experience where intuition replaces stagnant concepts. Until we have achieved a clear and truthful understanding of the laws underlying our three-dimensional world, we can't make sense out of or really experience higher dimensions.

From our "double thread," two-commandment view-point, the mystical represents the "love of God" commandment and the psychological the "love of neighbor." Both an enlightened psychologist and a mystic will tell us in substance, if not in fact, that we are made in the image of God, with which we would agree. Both will tell us that we have a shell of false identity built up by family, social conditioning, and education, but then the psychologist and the mystic will part company.

The psychologist will attempt to get rid of the false identity by pealing it off layer by layer in order to communicate with the true self, while the mystic will say, "Let's not think of or accept the past, the false identities. Instead, let's experience who you really are in truth." In other words, the mystic would refuse to accept the lie as a way of getting at the truth and a psychologist would accept the lie, the nature of error, and try to dissolve it in order to get to the truth.

If you are really clear about what you are doing, and if you have the capacity to see both the true infinite spiritual identity and the limited or false human one, you can be both a mystic and a psychologist. It's difficult but it can be done. You can be aware when you are at the psychological level and hang on to a realization of the spiritual identity at the same time.

The catch is that in working psychologically with the false identity, it is easy to start believing in limitation, that the human concept is the truth, thereby anchoring the persons to "this world." In reverse, when you are working mystically, the only way you help people is by refusing to believe for a second that they are anything but their true Christ selves.

Paradoxically, it is through reasoning, we come to an understanding of the relative nature of existence, but completeness is attained only when all conceptual thought and all word-consciousness has come to rest.

On the other hand, anyone who believes that the suppression of thought or of intellect is neccessary in order to experience enlightenment has painted himself into a corner. If we had no intellect, could not go beyond it or overcome it, we would never master it. Only what we master is our own. Intuition or the mystical experience is neccessary for transcending the intellect and the intellect is neccessary for transcending confusion and ignorance.

Many have believed that we have to be one way or the other, either psychological or mystical, and have created a division. Remember, the secret of the two commandments is that you have to be aware of an apparent duality in order to arrive at a true oneness or union, a union of the flesh and the spirit.

What I am underlining is that the first communication commandment (the love of God) represents mysticism or the fourth dimension and the second commandment (the love of neighbor) represents psychology or the third dimension approach. The first applies to communicating with our God self and the second communicating with our earth self. Communication is a two-way street. That's why we are given two commandments instead of one. When both are successful, they meet, communicate, and we are like unto each other.

When we look at the New Testament, we see that Jesus not only gave us this double approach but he began his teaching with mental or psychological instructions such as the Sermon on the Mount and led into the mystical experience.

Back in the fifties I heard, "Do you know who are going to finally heal all the physical and mental problems? It won't be the spiritual teachers or healers as we know them today. It will be the doctors and the psychologists." It said that at the moment the psychotherapists didn't have a clue and that they couldn't heal anything but that they would eventually search for and find mystical truths, take them over, and heal the world with them. I see it happening.

Many people need mental or psychyological help in order to get to the point where they can communicate with themselves. Then the mystic can help them communicate with God, their true identity.

An enlightened psychologist has the capacity to understand the spiritual nature of their client as well as the human. He or she can offer immediate help in order to create the space for a transformation of consciousness to take place. But, that can be like salve on a sore. The effectiveness of a mental approach is limited and often only works temporarily. Salve deals with symptoms, not causes.

What I have found, however, which has been an all-important help to me in keeping the communication lines open, is that I can stay on track if I can consciously recognize and be aware when I am at the psychological, mental feeling level and be aware when I am tuned in to the fourth dimensional mystical level and not confuse the two. That's how the "double thread" operates.

The person who is merely the slave of the outer world of circumstances over which he has no control, who lets every thing take possession of him, is as little capable of experiencing his mystical being as the one who is indifferent and unfeeling, allowing nothing to enter his heart. The first one loses himself in a miasma of ignorance; the second one is like someone who has a million dollars in the bank but doesn't know how to write a check.

Complements

Complements are another important "double thread" clue. This came together for me in practical terms one day when I was sitting on a mountaintop in Santa Barbara meditating. An idea came to me. It was one of the most down-to-earth practical things I had ever learned. If anything closes the gap between the infinite and the finite, it is this principle: *At the world level, everything needs a complement to complete it.*

Absolutes, as I said, do not stand alone at the level of "this world." On earth, they need complements to make them work. For instance, experience is a wonderful thing but if there isn't any knowledge of what has been experienced, it is valueless and wasted. Knowledge is wonderful but unless it is experienced empirically, it is sterile as well; so the complement of knowledge is experience and vice versa.

If intuition is not complemented by thought, it cannot have any significant influence upon our lives because nothing has power if it isn't directed. Nevertheless, thoughts which remain solely intellectual must be complemented by direct experience if they are to have the power to transform our lives and reveal our true beings.

The feminine needs to complement the masculine for each of us to be a whole person whether the two aspects are within one's own self or in a male-female relationship. No one stands alone. We all need some complement to complete us in our finite nature. I of my own self as a human being can do nothing but if I am complemented by my Father, I can do all things. In reverse, if God is my complement, I am His. The universal requires the individual as its complement and the divine requires the human in order to express itself.

Practically, whenever we contemplate anything that we wish to do or accomplish, if we figure out what is needed in order to complement our wish, we have a fighting chance of achieving it. Whenever I have a plan or a projection, I ask myself, "What does this need to complete it? What is the other side?" Everything finite, every concept, every act needs a complement to be whole.

The Mirror Image

The next thing we have to ask ourselves is, "What am I communicating?" After I had spent years studying the illusory nature of human existence, I was once at my home in Texas when I heard a member of my family refer to the evils of life as the realities. She said, "You have to face reality," meaning that facing hardship was facing reality. I responded, "No. What you call reality is a mirror image of reality. Reality is the opposite of what this world shows as the truth."

When I got into the business world, I soon learned that most things were the opposite of how they appeared. "Honest John" was probably the biggest crook in town. Peace treaties in which everyone was happy were the most fragile. In my theater life, I found that if there was a fault in a script, instead of fighting it, I should use it and turn it into a virtue. To hold your breath is to lose it.

In my spiritual life, this principle of reversal worked as well. When I could remind myself to reverse the image, distasteful things often turned out to be treasures.

For there to be a mirror image, there has to be a true image, something that actually is, that has form and shape. There is also the illusion which you see when you look into a mirror. In the mirror image, everything closely resembles reality. It looks the same, has the same shape, same size, same color but in actuality it is a lie in that it is an image, a symbol of the truth. Everything in the mirror image is in reverse—it's backward. But there has to be something real that does exist in order for a lie to exist about it. So we can take courage by knowing that behind every difficulty is a truth, a truth that has been reversed. Our first commandment self, our spiritual being, is the reality and our second commandment self, our neighbor self, is just a reflection of our true being. We do have both and if we can understand the difference, we can communicate truth-fully.

If you ever try to write while looking in a mirror, you will realize how confused you can get. Nothing comes out like you want it to. Your hand keeps moving in the opposite direction. Nothing comes out legibly until you practice and practice writing to the point where you can deal with the mirror image and automatically reverse it so that things come out truly. The same happens in our lives. We can reverse the image with practice. It takes hard work, time, and a constant awareness of the illusionary nature of the mirror image. That's another way of saying things come out right when we constantly exercise righteous judgment.

In the human scene, there are good and bad people, there is a power apart from God. That's the mirror image but in "My kingdom" the reverse is true. There are no people at all, as such, but rather everything is God appearing "as" people, as nature, as all the forms we see.

Of course, we see people. It's stupid to believe, as some do, that we can live without being aware that there are what appear as good and evil people. It is possible, though, to simultaneously be aware of the mirror image and not lose sight of the true being which is the reverse of what we see with our eyes.

So to get down to the nitty gritty of self, in a way there are two of me. One is real, the Christ, the son of the divine cause; the other is its mirror image, the psychological me. As long as there is one, there is the other. As long as I love one to the exclusion of the other, I hate the other. But when I realize that love means the communication of truth, I respond to both the same way. I see them for what they are. I see my true self as an embodiment of God. I also see my limited self as a backward mirror image of my truth; and I am, therefore, reminded by it of my truth.

Many of our greatest saints were our greatest sinners until they reversed their images: St. Augustine and St. Paul, for instance. In other words, because their truth was so vital, their mirror image reflected their strength in equal reversed negativity. We all know people whose mirror images appear most powerfully. They are probably our potentially greatest saints.

You know what happens when the mirror image and the object come together. When they do, they are communicating and there is no more reverse image because the two are one, the gap is closed. When the psychological and the mystical come together and are in total harmony, they are the same, neither one nor the other.

Our awareness, how we communicate, determines the world in which we live or how the universe appears to us. Nothing in itself is either one or another. We are always faced with a mirror-like reflection and if we view it with the impartiality of a mirror, we will become unaffected by the images our mind observes. We see what the Buddhists call our "essential nature" which is not either/or but the pure being on which all images are reflected.

Do you hear what I am saying? I thank God for my mirror image. That image I see in the mirror isn't truth but the only way I appear on earth is through the mirror, like Alice in Wonderland, so I can exist harmoniously as a mirror image as long as I translate it, reverse it, and know the image only symbolizes my true being.

The Priority Principle

There's another and all-important communication secret hidden in Jesus's two commandments. Like most profound truths, it is so subtle that for years I missed it. Yet without a constant and conscious awareness of this truth, the "double thread" doesn't work and our whole world could easily destroy itself.

Despite the countless times I read Chapter 22 of Matthew, where Jesus boiled down the whole law into the two commandments, I missed the small print. After Jesus said, "Thou shalt love the Lord thy God with all thy heart, and with all thy soul, and with all thy mind," He added, "This is the *first and great* commandment." In saying that, He was giving us a priority. He was giving us an order by which we should approach or communicate with life. By telling us to put God first, we are given a yardstick to measure our actions with.

Whenever we put material achievements before the spirit, we have reversed the priority and God isn't loved first. The "double thread" approach includes loving both materiality and spirituality but if the priority is not in order, it doesn't work.

When I look back over my life, I can see that if I had understood this priority, many of my past dilemmas would have been resolved. In the beginning, when I was studying all the world's religions trying to find universal truth, I realized that every religion included the same truths. Yet when I heard people say, "We are all saying the same thing," I felt something wasn't quite right. It took years before I realized what the difference was: different religions place the emphasis in different places. They don't have the same set of priorities, and the order in which we put or communicate ideas influences everything that follows.

For instance, we might have the ingredients needed to bake a cake but there is a priority of ingredients. We start with one, then add the next, and each follows the one before. The sequence dictates the quality or success of the final cake as it comes out of the oven. Those who reverse or have the wrong sequence of priorities fail.

When I realized the place and importance of emphasis, I was able to resolve a confusion I had maintained about my relationship to Joel's teachings. I knew that in his writings, at one place or another, I could find corroboration for everything I believed or wrote about and yet there was a difference. The difference was that there were times when I placed the emphasis or priority differently. Though I put the spirit first, I tend to place a greater importance on the material than was appropriate at the time Joel was writing. Though I believe the first and most important commandment is that we love God, we need to have a greater awareness of how to love the material scene as well and not to reject it as so many metaphysicians tend to do.

When I became aware of the "priority principle," it helped me understand the beginning of the book of St. John, which is the basic premise of metaphysics. "In the beginning was the Word . . . And the Word was made flesh." First comes the Word, God, the creative principle. After that, the flesh follows. First we invision, image, and then the material manifestation follows.

To use the cake analogy again, first we decide to make a cake. We image the cake. Perhaps we get a cookbook to help us image the cake, but then we get the ingredients and finally a material cake appears. The important moment is the moment the image takes place. The perfection of the image and the order of priority dictate the quality of the cake.

This priority of putting cause (God) first also helped me resolve a great deal of my personal guilt. This basic guilt is symbolized in the "fall of man" myth. I have always felt something was wrong with the belief that mankind was once perfect, then made a mistake, fell, and is now being punished for it. That theory places guilt on all humankind. Now I have another way of looking at it which allows us to go further in perfecting ourselves and, at the same time, eliminates the guilt.

The perfect concept or idea of humankind came into being eons ago. That was the Word. It is just taking this long for the perfect form to be manifested. We are not perfectly formed yet. We are the embodiment of that perfect idea on its way to perfect manifestation.

That reminds me of a statement I saw on a boy's T-shirt that illustrated the "priority principle": "Be patient with me. God isn't finished yet." First God and then form. Put cause before effects.

Jesus explained this priority in many different ways. The Mary and Martha story is a good example. Mary was sitting at Jesus's feet caring more about her spiritual appetite while Martha was doing all the housework and preparing material food. When Martha complained, Jesus didn't condemn her but rather suggested, "Mary hath chosen the better part." He let Martha know that spiritual food should take priority over chores.

Cause, Then Effect

When I began writing *The Gospel of Relativity*, I faced the dilemma of how to warn people about the possibility of destroying our world without increasing fear or being negative. I started the book with a happy story about the end of the world as we know it, a kind of futuristic parable. I wanted to say that we can indeed save the world and cure all its problems, not by finding more powerful or greater material solutions but rather by getting our priorities straight, by putting the spiritual solution before the material one.

You see, true cause, being spirit, is invisible. You can't see it. True cause is what gives us the ability to image and create new forms. Everything we see, touch, taste, and smell in the visible world has already been created. They are all effects. They are all the results of our invisible ability to create. We can overcome addiction, negate the alarming prognostications of disaster we read, become free of dependency on any person, place, or thing because we can simply reverse priority. We can once more put Spirit first and break the illusion that there is cause in effects.

When we realize that there is only one source, it is easy to keep the priority of God in the forefront. That's why I always get hot under the collar when people overcompliment me or claim that there are such people as ascended masters. They show that they are seeing effects as causes. There is only one source, one master teacher; it is God from whom all ideas or truths are drawn by anyone who voices truth.

On earth, there are costumes and mantles people wear, which represent states of consciousness. If we are attracted to a particular teacher or leader, it is because we are attracted to the state of consciousness he or she is inhabiting. We are right to honor that state of consciousness, but if we confuse it with the person, with an effect, we have our priorities wrong. We should love and honor the one who wears the mantle but not in such a way as to put anything before God.

This is why I like the "double thread" approach. It means I can thoroughly enjoy and use effects of all kinds. I can eat healthily, I can love my teachers, I can rejoice in meeting with other people. I can have it all and still have dominion when I have my priorities right and put God first in all circumstances.

Thingness is the opposite of livingness. There's a simple rule you can follow if you feel in danger of losing dominion or becoming dependent on anyone or anything: *whenever anything comes between you and God, drop it.*

If anything seems neccessary to someone, it has come between that one and God. That means that person has reversed the priority. Those who believe they have to go to a particular teacher in order to find God are in danger of putting their teacher between themselves and God. Whenever people believe that they have to go to a particular place to find God, that place can come between themselves and God. Whenever they think that a particular discipline is neccessary, then that discipline can reverse the priority and become more important than God.

The wonderful fact is that Jesus told us that there is something we can do about it. He said, "This kind goeth not out but by prayer and fasting." By prayer and fasting, we can reestablish the right priorities.

Fasting doesn't mean just fasting from food. It means fasting from anything that has come between us and God. Sometimes we need to fast from people, from work, even from meditation, if it becomes an addiction, or if we depend on it.

Fasts work because they break the law—the law of materiality. The law may say, for instance, that we have to eat three meals a day. If we fast, we find that the law isn't true. Fasts prove we are not dependent on anything in the visible world, that spirit comes first.

Self-Reliance

When we communicate spirit first, we are putting self-reliance first, with a capital "S". Emerson wrote his classic essay, "Self-reliance" in an attempt to forestall the possible reversal of priorities that he saw our country was heading toward, as we became more dependent on our technology and less dependent on the spirit within ourselves.

Emerson realized that America had led the world in creating a fantastic technology which could ultimately free the world, but there was the possibility that we might become imprisoned by the very "things" we had created and in turn lose our self-reliance. Self-reliance is invisible; it is a spiritual matter. It is a matter of communicating the truth of being to ourselves. When we become dependent on our visible creations, we have reversed our priorities and are no longer communicating with our God selves.

The Latin root word for "reliance" is "religare" which means "to tie back" ("re" back and "ligare" to tie). If so, then self-reliance means to tie back to the God within ourselves. What is suprising but significant, is that the word "religion" also comes from the root word "religare." In other words, the goal of religion is, or should be, to arrive at a state of self-reliance where we have returned to the priority of putting spirit before effects. Religion should tie the two commandments together in divine order.

THREE

The Total Self

As long as you are still linear about your own identity, your communications have to be limited and inadequate. In the early years, I spent so much time trying to communicate with God that I didn't realize I couldn't do that until I learned to communicate with my self, or, I should say, "my selves."

The words "know thyself" were inscribed over the entrance to a Greek temple thousands of years ago, but it has only been in the last thirty years that so many people have jumped on the bandwagon and created the current rash of self-awareness or self-potential groups. It has finally been realized that most people don't know how to communicate with their own capacities, talents, and abilities, and therefore couldn't operate successfully until they explored and recognized who they really were. Unfortunately most of those who advocated self-awareness courses mistakenly believed that discovering one's self meant discovering one's ego. Ego is only one limited aspect of our being. We are really a whole bunch of different people wrapped up under one skin. We are infinite and can't say we know ourselves until we experience our total being.

To close the gap between our multi-dimensional being and our ego concept of self, we need a new mental language. The language we need won't be new in terms of new words, because words can always be conditioned and distorted, but in the sense of a new way of thinking or conceiving of identity as an extended multi-dimensional logic. This new logic will be as different from the Aristotelian "*A*, therefore *B*, therefore *C*" logic as Einstein's theory of relativity was from all mathematical concepts that preceded it.

Our Western logic moves in a straight line from one concept to another while Eastern logic circles around the subject. Our Western head-on approach leads to a speedier, narrower, and more judgmental conclusion. The Eastern approach circles around, creating a multi-dimensional confusion that, though all-embracing, tends to reject specific action. If we could create a new, fluid, "double thread" awareness which combined the two, we could see divinity in individual humanity.

I lost one of my most beloved friends because I wasn't able to communicate this in-depth concept of my own multi-dimensional nature. He got exasperated with me one day and said, "You are a hypocrite. One minute you are all sweetness and light, all spiritually motivated, and at the next moment, when it is more convenient for you, you are materialistic and worldly." I was just being my "double thread" self, but at that point I wasn't clearly communicating the pantheon of my identities.

I wish I could have a red light bulb growing out of one side of my head and a blue one out of the other side. Then I could explain that when the red one is on, I am coming from my material sense and when the blue one is on, from my spiritual awareness. Most of us switch back and forth but we either don't realize it or don't give ourselves permission. In my early life, I was confused and felt that something was wrong with me because I had so many apparently contradictory feelings at the same time. I thought I was supposed to be one way, loving and spiritual, all the time. I was tricked by a belief in the necessity of consistency.

Consistency and Crystallization

Consistency is another one of those hypnotic assumptions which keeps us in darkness. Through consistency we create a crust of prejudices and useless concepts which had meaning in the past but is now yesterday's manna. That which has frozen into a form belongs to the past and to death; if we cling to it out of habit, we are opting for death.

Absoluteness, perfectionism, and consistency are sister traps. As I said, there are no absolutes in living a creative human existence. I can imprison a seed in a bottle, seal it up, and it will be perfect, consistent, and secure for centuries. But it will also be dead and uncreative. The seed has to die to be born again in order to grow into a plant, inconsistent in form, alive. Security is death. Death is actually just a stage in the transitions of life.

Many people sit at the feet of a master until one day they see their master be inconsistent or act humanly. Then the disciples run screaming. That's why some teachers won't let their students get close to them. They realize that sooner or later their humanity will show in one way or another and they are afraid their students will be confused. If they understood their own "double thread" nature and were secure enough to explain it, they wouldn't have that problem.

I am not a person with just one identity. I am a cluster of identities and each must have its day. What's more, I am not just body, mind, and spirit. As commonly conceived, that holistic approach is too limiting. If I get stuck in any one level, just seeing myself as a person, I've crystallized. I've put myself in a bottle. I'm dead.

I've always felt that the only death in life is crystallization or consistency. People can crystallize at any age. I've known twenty year olds who have crystallized their identities. Whenever young people say they know what they want to do with their lives, I worry about them. They should want to do all kinds of things, have a number of different professions, be a number of different people. Whenever any of us get stuck in just a few levels of our identity, we are like an automobile that isn't running on all its cylinders. We are infinite and shouldn't be satisfied unless we express all of our infinity. Perhaps that is why Thomas Jefferson said we should have a revolution every ten years—to break up the crystallization.

More and more people are becoming dissatisfied with being stuck in one job consistently doing the same thing over and over. That's one of the reasons so many people today have multiple jobs. That's also why more and more women are dissatisfied with being stuck in the home, consistently limited to housework. They have realized that they are infinite beings able to perform many professions and they wish to express their infinity without crystallizing in one spot.

The desire to be inconsistent and to keep from crystallizing isn't a character fault. It's a help. When we accept the fact that we are infinite and able to succeed in many areas, we can be more content doing the job we are doing at the moment because we know that we won't have to be limited indefinitely as the life process moves on.

By the same token, when the life process does break up the crystallization for us, it is a blessing. Losing a job, or being offered a new one out of the blue; going through a divorce or getting married; even the death of a loved one is probably the divine process pushing us out of the prison of consistency or crystallization.

Sometimes I have suprised myself by deliberately precipitating an argument or disagreement within a close relationship and have been confused as to the reason. I now realize that unconsciously I was stirring things up in order to keep the relationship from crystallizing. Consistency precludes spontaneity.

If life doesn't break up the crystallization for us, sometimes we have to do it ourselves. It was the danger of crystallizing which pushed me into leaving Key West in my late forties. I was uniquely comfortable, a VIP in a small but exciting pond. The Chamber of Commerce had made me Citizen of the Year, editorials in the paper proclaimed my contribution to the city for having created the successful Key West Hand Print Fabrics factory, and for having started the Old Island Restoration Society, but something within me knew I wasn't "there" yet. I had more to learn and experience. I needed to stretch further; so I deliberately sold my home, burned my bridges, and moved on.

This has happened to me a number of times in big and small ways. When things are too good for too long, I say, "OK, God, throw some more at me. I don't want to stop growing until I am totally there. I want to do it all in this lifetime." I'll admit, however, that before long I start screaming, "That's enough. That's enough. Let up."

The Blessing of Obsolescence

The human being side of us wants to crystallize. We believe that we will survive if we are secure. That's why we cling to the first law of human nature, survival. But if we want to know how to keep from freezing up, we should start appreciating obsolesence.

In order to die daily to yesterday's concepts or limitations, we have to realize that everything, every teaching, every concept from yesterday is already obsolete. I'm not kidding. Even what you are reading at this moment will be obsolete the moment after you have read it, or the moment you have added the slightest new dimension to it from your own experience. Yesterday is obsolete. That's what future shock is, the shock of obsolescence brought on by the communications explosion.

In the past, we adjusted to change, as I stated in *The Gospel of Relativity*. When something new came along, we tried to fit it in with the old, but today change is a way of life. The changes are coming so fast that we now have to feed on change, enjoy it, even demand it. In fact, it is spiritual to enjoy change. It demands trust. It means our dependency isn't on visible security. When we welcome change, it means we are not leaning on our hard won knowledge, on yesterday's magic, or even on our loved and honored teachers.

Besides, it's a real misnomer for disciples to say they are teaching their teachers' teaching. They can't possibly; only the initial teacher can. Each disciple can only teach his or her own consciousness which may be greatly based on the teacher's but the disciple's interpretation is uniquely his or her own; no two are alike and, what's more, each is constantly new.

Not long before Joel died, he told me that within ten years his teaching would not be his teaching because it would be frozen into the words he had left it in and that, to be a living message, it would have to continue to grow, change and be put into new words.

I was alone with Joel the day before he left the United States to visit England, where he passed on. He suddenly asked me, in premonition of his death, I suspect, "Walter, when are you going to teach?" I said, "Joel, I will never teach the Infinite Way. (That's what he called his message.) I can't. Only you can. I can only voice my own consciousness, whatever that is. But I promise I will share whatever I have with whoever wants it." He jumped up, shook my hand up and down, and said, "Thank you, thank you, thank you," almost like saying, "Thank God. Someone has heard me."

Wait a minute, I didn't say your pet past beliefs are valueless. Heavens, no. If you are closer to the awareness of an ultimate truth than ever before, it is because of all that has brought you to where you are now. Every bit of the past has contributed to the *total* you, but this extraordinary explosion of growth or change taking place has added new dimensions of awareness daily and that makes whatever went before obsolete, not valueless, but obsolete.

Sure, we can be aware of all the old that is incorporated in the new and appreciate that fact, but if we think that our guru or treasured teaching possess *all* the truth, why are we still searching? Why did our teachers think they had to add to their teachers' teachings?

If we refuse to believe that we can go beyond the past, even beyond our teachers, it is because we don't love ourselves enough to step out into the invisible, to accept obsolescence, and go beyond. Until we do, the next level can't be reached. Jump!

Total-ism

Come to think of it, this biographical map of my own evolution around which I keep jumping, parallels a lot of what was taking place simultaneously in the collective consciousness during the time and space in which my own development was proceeding. My concept of total being turned into an "-ism" for me in the late sixties when communes were the popular attraction for everyone. At that time, many people were becoming aware of Findhorn, that extraordinary community in the north of Scotland where they started out communing with the Devas and raising forty-pound cabbages on a sand spit, and graduated into raising people's consciousness.

Well, I had spoken at Findhorn several times before but this time I was to give a major address for their annual whole earth conference. Naturally, being in such a community, community was on my mind, and in meditation I suddenly heard what the real value in experiencing life in a community was. We as individuals are no different from a community. I am a whole community of identities or dimensions and the same principles used in successfully organizing and getting a community of people to communicate are the ones that can help the community of my own identities organize and communicate within myself.

On the day of my address, I was meditating on how I could put my feelings about the need to live "totally" into words and an analogy popped into my head which has been a great help ever since. I call it "totalism." I'd like to share it.

I realized that just as our scientists tell us that water, ice, steam, and vapor are all H_2O, nothing but hydrogen and oxygen, our teachers or priests tell us that everything we see is God, nothing but God appearing. Well, both the theories of God and H_2O are abstractions. I can't relate to anything I haven't experienced. As a human being I can think about abstractions but can't really identify with them. However, I have experienced the different forms H_2O has taken. I can drink water, I can feel the cold of ice, I can sweat in steam.

What's more, though ice, water, and steam are all H_2O and nothing but H_2O, they take dramatically different forms. What neither scientists nor my teachers have told me is that each dimension, each level of being, has its own laws. I don't drink with an ice pick. Cups belong to the water level but are useless for steam.

I believe in my minister, teacher, or guru. They are beautiful persons. I trust them. They tell me that ice picks are good for H_2O so I rush out and try to chop a cup of water and fail—and I feel guilty. Unfortunately, they either don't know or haven't told me that

I am a multi-dimensional person and that there are different laws for each level of my total being. Though they are all one substance, each dimension has different laws operating it.

Each plane has its own laws and its own problems. The methods which are helpful toward a solution in one case can become a hinderance in another. Often if we try to use logic to see one level in terms of another, we are dragged back into a third dimensional approach to life. The best we can do is to observe a kind of parallelism or coexistence. Carl Jung attempted to explain God as a multi-dimensional being by advocating an awareness of synchronistic being.

In attempting to live as a multi-dimensional being, the best possible thing I can do is to be like water. I boil the water because when I lift the consciousness of the water to the boiling point, it purifies the water. Boiling would be the equivalent of a person arriving at illumination, samadhi, nirvana, or masterhood. When you arrive at that spiritual boiling point, your soul is purified. On the other hand, there are a number of spiritual guides who imply it is admirable to boil all the time. That's ridiculous. You'd be just like water. You'd evaporate.

Instead, we should leave no stone unturned in learning how to make our contact with spirit because in that way we purify our souls. But then we should have the courage and integrity to cool the water down so that we can enter the world, the market place, and wash babies with it, water plants with it, drink it, and eventually even freeze it to preserve vegetables. As a matter of fact, when you get too spiritual about mundane things, you may scald them with judgment.

Carlos Castañeda put it succinctly in *Tales of Power*. He said that after we have experienced our total identity, we should be "impeccable" warriors. He claimed that to be a warrior and to be impeccable, we have to courageously operate at all of our different identities with the purity of each level and not ignore any. If we are either afraid to be human, afraid to feel, afraid to be involved or afraid to surrender to pure spirit, we can't be warriors in this battle aimed at communicating freedom to those hypnotized by the forces of darkness. And if we can't communicate with our divinity, we have no strength with which to fight for our truth.

Another thing we have to realize in our quest for totalism is that everything—absolutely everything and every feeling—has a right use and a right place. Oil may seem to pollute water. To purify water, we have to skim off the oil, but that doesn't mean that oil isn't good in itself. It is valuable when it is burned in a lamp. The problem isn't with the oil. The oil isn't to be blamed for polluting the water. Ignorance is. The problem is that out of ignorance or wrong communication the oil has been placed where it doesn't belong. It's the same about all your own feelings, talents, abilities, and energies. There is a place, a time, a purpose and a right function for any feeling or thought.

In fact, there is only a degree of difference between levels. At 33 degrees you have water. At 32 degrees you begin to have ice. The difference between a master and a student is not an enormous gap. Your master level and your human level are just a degree apart.

This H_2O analogy not only helped me get rid of guilt at those times when I was confusing my different dimensions but it also gave me the cluster sense of my identity so that I wasn't linear about myself. I found that if I choose—and this is where free will comes in— I could stop whatever I was doing, tune in to whatever level I was currently at, communicate, see if what I was doing was appropriate, and if not, transmute it into the right level through either meditation or intuition.

Another example. When people ask me "How do you pray?" I always answer, "Which me are you talking about?" If you come to the door at five in the morning, I will screw up my face, and growl, "What da ya want?" But if you come at around nine o'clock when I have had a nice meditation and a cup of coffee, I will come to the door, smile, and croon, "Yes, dear, what can I do for you?" I have different ways of praying depending on whatever level I am at. Don't we all? This is what I mean about the "double thread" approach.

You become a total person by *incorporation*, not *elimination*. You communicate by incorporating, not eliminating.

The Wave and the Particle

There's a catch here. I started this chapter saying it was about how I learned to communicate with my total being but there's a difference between communicating with each separate identity and with the total identity. The divine paradox is that the total "I am" is different from all the pieces that make it up.

Most people wander around in their various human identities searching for their divine One, but oneness can't be seen. It can only be experienced. They never find it because they are looking for it in finite terms. I think I did it the other way around. Experiencing my God self came fairly easily but I didn't communicate with my confused human parts until totalism showed me a place for each and how the whole broke down into the pieces.

Joseph Chilton Pearce demystified the supernatural relationship between our human selves and our God selves and made it scientifically supranatural rather than supernatural when he equated the difference between our identities in terms of quantum physics. I see his analysis of the wave-particle aspect of energy as similar to the two commandments—the wave as God and the particle as neighbor. He explained that all matter is energy formed but we can't understand matter in terms of energy or vice versa; neither can we understand God in terms of man or vice versa. He wrote:

> The wave-particle dilemma in physics is analogous to the difference between the biological and post-biological states of mind. Physicists say both wave and particle states of energy are needed to explain a phenomenon, yet the two—wave and particle—are mutually exclusive. You can observe one or the other but not both at the same time. Physicists speak of wave energy as non-localized; it has no time-space characteristics and so doesn't exist in the same sense that physical matter exists. The particle, or physical matter, is localized energy; it has a location in time and space. Yet this localized, fixed energy is a restricted way of looking at the non-localized or unrestricted energy. Non-localized energy is an unrestricted field of possibility from which the particle of matter manifests. For the particle to manifest, the field's open potential collapses to that single expression of the particle; and no field is then manifested. For the field to manifest, the particle must respond to its wave form at which point it cannot exist in its localized way.

The Hindus say the same in describing God. They say, "If you can name it, it isn't." God, the wave, can be experienced but it can't be voiced. The minute you voice anything, you turn it into a particle, a thing. You break it off from the whole. You may talk of the qualities of God but none of them are all of God, therefore none is an accurate and complete experience of God. But this wave/particle theory, as Pearce says, "allows us to enter into play of the dynamics between reality and possibility."

In simpler terms, if you ever hear me say, "I am God," lock me up. When I am talking, I am at my particle level and that is limited. But if you could crawl into my meditation when I have reached that boiling point, where I have dropped all sense of ego self, you might hear me internally say, "I and my Father are one." At that moment, I am tuned in to my wave self.

The statement, "God is individual being," translates, "The wave manifests as the particle." Until I can experience the fact that God is my individual being, I haven't left the particle level of my being. Until I can experience your waveness, I haven't loved you with God's love, with the first commandment. To love you as a person is to appreciate your particle expression but to love you with God's love is to experience your waveness.

It is never one or the other but, unfortunately, we can't communicate the same way we do with one as we do with the other. I can experience your divinity but I can't think of it. I can see your body under a microscope, but I can't touch your spirit with my hands.

The divine paradox and our human problem as particle beings is that the whole is indeed more than the sum of its parts but the part receives its meaning from the whole. The wave continues no matter what, but if the particle is detached from the totality of the universe, it becomes a nonentity. The particle that becomes constantly conscious of its connection to the wave becomes what we call a "saint." Yet individuation becomes neccessary in order for us to become consciously aware of our universality. The wave cannot be experienced except by individuals and yet individuals only have meaning because of their relations to the universal.

The wave and the particle, universality and individuality, are not exclusive or opposite to each other but are the complements, the poles that are mutually dependent. That's why we cannot attain union by thinking we can destroy our individuality. Our job is to conceive of our individuality as self rather than egotism.

This "double thread" approach is also why Jesus was so confusing at times. At one moment, He would say, "The Son can do nothing of himself," and "Why callest thou me good?" meaning "As a particle I am limited." And then at the next moment He would say, "He that hath seen me hath seen the Father," meaning, "See the particle and you see the wave."

When I came up with the belief that I was simultaneously both a limited particle and the omnipotent wave, it looked like a neat way for me to be able to excuse all my shortcomings. I may not have gotten away with that but it certainly helped me sleep happily at night.

The wave-particle theory also helps me understand and explain the difference between the so-called third dimension and the fourth. The third dimension represents the particle level and the fourth the wave level. I have my third-dimensional self which is totally different from my fourth-dimensional self, my unlimited unformed spirit. As ice and water are the same but different, so are the different vibrational levels of me.

Jesus, whose name was really Yeshua, wasn't called Christ until He got to that point where His fourth dimensional waveness was recognizable even through His particleness. After that, He was given the "double thread" name, Jesus Christ, in recognition of both His particle nature and His wave connection. We should do the same in recognition of each other's double nature. We should greet each other with, "Hello, Mary Christ. Hello, Bob Christ. Hello, Walter Christ."

We do have to keep in mind, though, that there is really only One. The "double thread" is only one thread but it is made up of two strands, the spiritual and the material. After all, a single strand thread isn't anywhere near as strong as a thread of similar size that is made up of two intertwined strands. When we look back, we can see that from the beginning, the fabric of our life has been woven by the woof and warp of our double nature. When the two are bonded in love, we are strong.

The Bonding Magic

Communication bonds. The magic of communication with either the parts of our own multi-dimensional nature or with the body of all humankind is the process of bonding. That's what love is: bonding. Bonding takes place when we really communicate. When two people love each other, they bond with each other. When we love God, we have been bonded with our wave self.

When my first book came out, the publisher called me a "modern mystic" on the dust jacket. My sister, who was a Methodist preacher's wife, had a fit. She thought that being a mystic meant sitting cross-legged contemplating my nose, if not my navel. I explained that the dictionary says a mystic is anyone who believes that "it is possible to achieve communion (communicate) with God through meditation and love." So those who believe it is possible for their particle selves to communicate with the wave source are mystics.

The odd thing is that you can be a mystic bonding with God and still not know how to bond with other particles. My ability to bond or communicate with God supplied me with the direction and ideas which made my life creatively successful. I didn't realize it then but the only way the real bonding takes place with anyone or anything is through the wave. I bonded with Goldsmith, Prabvananda, van Druten, and a few others but it was always because the mutual interest we shared was God, the spirit. I could bond because I wasn't trying to bond horizontally from particle to particle but rather vertically from particle to the wave which in turn resulted in a bonding with other particles which were also bonding through the wave.

Let me explain. Once we are ejected out into the world, we feel that our initial bond with God has been broken. We've been turned into a separate particle. We've experienced separation. A human being's initial bonding naturally takes place with his own mother from whom he came. Bonding with father doesn't come at first. At first, all our dependencies are fulfilled in the two-way bonding with our mothers. Our mothers bond with us because we came from them and we with them for the same reason. There is no other bonding quite like that of the mother and child.

All existential anxiety is the fear of not being able to bond. As we grow, we are increasingly tricked into believing we can bond horizontally from particle to particle. For a male, sex can become a substitute for bonding with mother, back to the womb. He feels that if he can reenter the womb, he will bond again. By occupying the womb, the female may subconsciously be identifying with the same bonding impulse. Behind every impulse we have, sexual or otherwise, is the desire to bond or communicate because true bonding is love. As a spiritually motivated sexual act is the flower of the communication of love, sex is or should be the result of bonding, not its cause.

When two people have sex without first making spiritual contact, they think they are bonding because in physical terms they can't get any closer. But unfortunatly, most of the time casual sex encounters are attempts to bond horizontally rather than vertically. Two people who think they are bonding because of their sexual attraction find that, when the glue of sexual desire wears thin, the bonding breaks. But when the bonding takes place vertically, through God, through an awareness of the waveness of each other, it lasts forever.

Sexual relation is the most intimate communication possible, but the same bonding process takes place in every encounter. For instance, I have a business problem. I sit down to meditate before taking any action. My intent is to stop seeing my problem from my finite particle level and experience my oneness with my wave consciousness. If I do contact the wave spiritual level, I bond with the persons I wish to do business with because they too are parts of the wave. If I can take my eyes off the horizontal particle level and make that contact, I will hear the proper steps to take, and by going through the wave to the particle level, success is certain.

In my Broadway producer days, every time the phone rang, I would silently say to myself, "Thank you, Father," as a way of contacting the wave before I answered the call. Every time I was interviewed on television, I closed my eyes for a moment and realized, "My oneness with God constitutes my oneness with all spiritual idea and being." That bonded me with everyone who was watching because, just as I am a particle which is part of the wave, so are they and we are communicating because of our oneness, not because of our separation, not horizontally but vertically.

One of the best explanations of how to bond that I have run across is the 15th century monk's treatise called, *The Cloud of Unknowing*. I read that little book every year for at least fifteen years before I realized it was a perfect explanation of the "double thread." In it, the author explains that the best we can do as our lower particle selves is to align our "intent" with the highest principles of love and service. This is the psychological neighbor commandment. Then, by grace, we may be able to pierce the cloud of unknowing, go beyond particle thought into the wave experience of our higher selves.

When that happens, it is like an airplane breaking the sound barrier. The closer your particle self gets to exploding into infinity, the bumpier the ride becomes, but once through the barrier, suddenly everything is calm and serene. You have arrived at the alpha wave. This can happen because the fourth or spiritual dimension is also a mirror image of our good intentions. When they come together, they bond and become one.

First, however, we must believe and accept the fact that, despite appearances, it is possible to experience the wave, the fourth dimension, God. We must accept that we, though human, can experience God. We can bond the flesh and the spirit.

Pearce also said, "The power of the bond is the arc across the gap of paradox." That arc breaks the law. It is grace— the magic bonding. Without it, bonding can't take place. Grace is the addition to the "double thread" which turns it into a trinity. It makes the three as One. We have the Father (wave), the Son (particle), and the Holy Spirit (bonding).

You see, we have the two commandments. The object is to bring these two, the wave and the particle, together and create the arc, the spark, the bonding which unites them. Whether they consciously know it or not, the desire people have to take communion is the desire to bond with God. The freedom they feel after they have taken communion is due to the bonding which has freed them to love. Communion represents the magic of bonding. It takes place whenever the particle communicates with the wave—when, through transubstantiation, the bread (the particle) becomes the wave (the body of Christ). We may not have consciously realized it but that is what the communion service at church is supposed to offer us, an opportunity to bond.

FOUR

Simultaneity

How's your juggling? As you may have noticed, I keep adding concepts and variations on the "double thread" theme expecting you to keep all the ideas in motion at the same time, not losing sight of any, seeing them all in a cluster relationship to each other.

I began the juggling act with my realization in Hawaii that nothing was either/or, that I was both man of earth and man of God, that these two were like unto each other but not the same. Then to make it simple, I lumped all the human sides together in the material, visible, speakable, conceptual world and labeled it the "psychological dimension," while the invisible, spiritually experience-able, but unthinkable side I called the "mystical." With this in mind, I had a communication handle with which to solve the identity dilemma I had found to be the basis of every problem.

Then I realized that the method of solving all my problems, spiritual or material, and the method for making the "double thread" approach work involves communication. When true communication takes place, totality is the result, bonding is the magic, and simultaneity is what makes it possible. Through simultaneity, we communicate. Juggling requires that you keep all these balls in the air simultaneously. I'm still stuck with using linear words, I have no other choice, but cluster is our aim. Keep juggling these concepts, feel what I am saying rather than think of it and in the end we will explode into an experience.

Our capacity for conscious simultaneity is still in its primitive state and we won't strengthen this capacity unless we become aware of it and exercise it. Fortunately, evolution takes place faster than we think. In just a few thousand years, a flicker of a second in geological time, we have evolved in amazing ways. The most important is in the area of consciousness.

Today, psychologists say that we are just now becoming conscious beings. They may be talking about being consciously aware, but consciousness goes way beyond awareness. As we become conscious, we split up our sense of identity and become aware that we are not only multi-dimensional beings, but that we are living many lives simultaneously.

Though I had a feel for simultaneity a long time ago, it wasn't until I had a surprising experience with a drug near the end of the sixties that I gained added perspective. I was then and still am heartily against the use of either mild or potent drugs as a means of accomplishing anything, but without having taken any at all, I had written a chapter on drugs in *The Ultimate Revolution*. Though my drug-experimenting young friends had validated what I wrote, I wanted to check it out for myself; so I decided to take one acid trip.

I found out from this one experience that drugs don't give you a spiritual experience. They give you a supersensual or supermaterial experience, perhaps a psychological one. At any rate, before that time I had "sensed" a number of my past incarnations in terms of consciousness but hadn't clothed them with any actual form, place, or material trappings. Well, this time I tuned in to an incarnation that took place a couple of thousand years ago. I pictured the hovel or home we were in, the clothes we wore, the looks on our faces, and felt as we felt. To my surprise, we were much more emotional and mentally clumsy then. Our minds were mush, not as sharp and facile as they are now. Our consciousness was basic and limited. We were highly superstitious and couldn't conceive of ourselves as anything other than just a body. We had no sense of simultaneity.

That experience reinforced my belief that evolution from the one-cell amoeba into the sophisticated humankind we are today has represented a steady growth in consciousness itself. Each stage potentially increases freedom from and command over our material existence. We are unable even now to comprehend capacities which we have not yet grown into, just as it is difficult for us now to identify with what we were like back in those more primitive days.

For instance, most insects have not yet developed three-dimensional sight. Their eyes are a series of sensors which are aware of motion as light passes over them. A bug moves its head back and forth and the result is that things in the distance do not seem to move as fast as things close up. When the bug gets nearer to an object, the object seems to move faster and that tells the bug to change direction. Try it. Hold a finger out in front of you, move your head from side to side, and you will notice that, as you move the finger closer to your eyes, it seems to move faster.

Well, up until now, our sense of time has been as primitive as a bug's sense of space. We have not yet developed to the point of fourth-dimensional time where simultaneity is not only taking place but becomes conscious, and until we do, simultaneity as a practical help isn't possible. Time is still linear to most people, despite the fact that mystics from centuries past have told us that time is not a reality as we generally conceive of it. Because Jesus understood simultaneity, He could say, "Before Abraham was I am." ✔

Today we are getting closer to an awareness of fourth-dimensional time because scientists such as Einstein have proved even mathematically that time is relative, not linear, and when we are able to sense the relative nature of time, simultaneity becomes a reality. And we are able to communicate in ways we never have before.

I took a big jump forward in my own search for self-love when I gave myself permission not only to be a number of different identities but to be them simultaneously. Often I had felt guilty when I experienced two different emotions at the same time. For instance, I was taught that if I loved someone, I couldn't simultanously hate that person. But I found that whenever I felt love for anyone, a tiny part of me also felt resistance to them. And I thought something was wrong with me. I thought that it was bad to have mixed feelings. It wasn't.

I am infinite, all inclusive. One me loves and yet the other me resents being dependent on anyone or anything. When I became free of the witch doctors' curse of absolutes, I realized that all emotions are contained within me simultaneously and I can choose to let the loving one be dominant. It's my choice. Simultaneity allows me to understand free will.

The old motion picture (and church) myth that boy meets girl, they fall in love, get married, and live happily ever after, has produced more poisonous guilt than you can imagine. Sometimes before the wedding bells have stopped ringing, boy or girl feels a tiny something like the opposite of love and believes he or she has failed. Their perfect love has been spoiled. They don't know there is no inconsistency or fault in experiencing different feelings simultaneously.

Most people think their spiritual lives are failures, because their humanity hasn't gone away. How silly. The goal isn't elimination but dominion. When the spiritual self is in the driver's seat, the human self is still in the back seat along for the ride. What's important is not who's included in the car but rather who is behind the steering wheel guiding the total.

As we are total beings we include both male and female impulses and include them simultaneously. Many men and women have tortured themselves with the fear of being homosexual because they have at some time or other felt an inkling of attraction to a member of their own sex. If they realized that everyone feels this to some degree because we all simultaneously include all feelings in our total being they wouldn't feel abnormal. In reverse, homosexuals create a sense of abnormality and limit themselves if they believe they are only able to be attracted to their own sex not realizing they potentially simultaneously have all feelings. After all, as we read in the Bible, the soul is androgynous, neither male or female but perhaps both.

Through polarity, made possible by simultaneity, dominion replaces elimination. We can choose which aspects of our being we wish to have dominion and direct the course of our lives. For instance, I saw a film on the training of seeing-eye dogs. The instructor stated that their goal was to train the dog out of its dogness so that it wouldn't rush off to the first fire hydrant it saw. That is similar to the idea that we should die daily to our humanness. Unfortunately some absolutists imply that in eliminating the dogness you have to kill the dog. No. A dog whose dogness has been overcome can lead the blind to safety. Through simultaneity dominion triumphs over elimination.

The capacity for simultaniety is a matter of relative time, the past, the future, and the present are all taking place *now*. There is no time but now, and it has nothing to do with past and future.

A simple way of realizing the effect our primitive linear sense of time has had on our lives is to recognize that it is impossible to have a worry or care in the world without getting out of the present now. Try it. Try to think of a problem and see if you are not thinking of a past mistake or are anticipating a future problem, neither of which is taking place at this second. If you regret a past action or contemplate a future one, you are involved in a fantasy because everything that isn't happening now is unreal in terms of the moment. So you see, our false primitive sense of linear time actually creates our sense of separation from God. All of your identities exist simultaneously now and none can be eliminated from your present being.

Again, the object is not to eliminate but to incorporate. The reason this was and is so important for me personally is that it gets rid of the belief that I must change. I can't. The belief that we can change is another one of those dark tricks that imprisons us in guilt. I can't be minus any of my simultaneous identities. By knowing this, I don't need to waste time trying to change; instead, I can spend that time profitably altering my priorities. Not myself, my priorities. I can place greater emphasis on that part of myself I had ignored. When I can accept the simultaneous nature of my total self, I can love myself because I no longer think I have to change. I can focus on my present totality.

It took me years to develop a conscious awareness of even a bit of simultaneity. I don't think any of us will rush out and achieve full realization of these powers right this minute, but if we can get a sense of our simultaneous identity, the process has begun. If you have any feel for what I have been saying, the capacity for experiencing God is already at work in you.

If we can break through the limitation of time sense and make even the beginnings of an awareness of simultaneity, we become free in some amazing areas. For example, we find ourselves able to stop judging not only ourselves but others. Judgment too involves linear time, time when something is not doing what we think it should be doing now. If we become aware that we are observing only one identity of a person and the other more desireable identities are there simultaneously only waiting to come out, we can be more patient. Rather than resist evil, we can encourage good. Rather than telling people they should change, we can help them express the good they already have included in their simultaneity.

The concept of simultaneity applies to our belief in God as well as in each other. The three words we most often use to describe God actually define simultaneity. "Omnipresence" is the simultaneity of presence, "omniscience" is the simultaneous availability of all knowledge, "omnipotence" is the simultaneity of all power.

Perhaps in the future, we will realize that in order to educate our children, we should enhance their capacity for intuition by teaching simultaneity. Intuition isn't possible without simultaneity. Simultaneity bridges time and joins the past and future with the present. Instead, education, as it is today, is exactly the opposite of simultaneity. It claims there is only one right way to be, one right way to think, or one right way to do a thing, not explaining that at the next moment what was right can be wrong. We teach young people that they should make up their minds who they are and what they want to do by the time they are in high school, instead of encouraging their infinite simultaneous potential. We won't get rid of guilt until we teach simultaneity. Or, I should say, we won't teach people how to love themselves until we do.

The Dilemma of Sin

The word "sin" comes from a word in Greek archery meaning "to fall short of the mark." When an arrow has fallen short of the target, it has "sinned." That's all sin is, falling short of the mark. Sin isn't a moral issue.

Like the "fall of man" myth, I wrestled with the concept of "original sin" and rebelled at the guilt trip it laid on me as though I was being punished for something I had done. Finally I realized that original sin was an explanation of a dilemma we all have by just being born. We each have finite bodies but we are able to comprehend infinity. In our finiteness, we can never achieve the infinite perfection we can conceive. We, as finite beings, naturally fall short of our infinite simultaneous nature. That's good. It keeps us reaching out to the total, to God.

If we didn't sense our infinity, we wouldn't try to create anything. When we are in violation of the laws of the particular dimension at which we are operating, we are falling short at that dimension, not at our other dimensions.

As I said in the part on totalism, each level has its own laws. Ultimately anything that causes us to fall short of our true being is a sin. Fortunately, we are all sinners or we would never wake up to who we really are. In this respect, sin is our friend because it forces us to strengthen, grow, try again and again until we find the right principle for each level and no longer fall short in any. It is our nature to stretch toward infinity.

To tell someone he is a sinner just because he missed at one dimension is as ridiculous as telling a child he is a failure in school because he failed in math when he had simultaneously made "A" in English, "A" in history, "A" in science, and "A" in social studies. Being out of balance in a moving universe is not the sin; to judge all levels just because one level is out of balance is the sin.

A personal example—a simple one but it demonstrates the principle. Frankly, my appetite is to luxuriate at the impersonal inner mystical level as much of the time as I can, but just yesterday I got a call from someone who was obviously at a personal level of need. Selfishly I did not shift gears and immediately respond to him at the level from which he was coming. He didn't tell me he was seeking help but I should have known. I was unwilling at that moment to let go of where I was and shift from the impersonal to the personal. That was a sin, a falling short of my "double thread" response-ability to love at the personal level as well as at the mystical. The friend was asking for bread and I offered a stone.

Shortly after I had hung up the phone, I felt a vibration telling me I had fallen short somewhere. Once I had tuned in, I realized what I had done. I was able to shift gears, to call my friend, and to communicate at the level at which my friend was asking for help and was able to redress the shortcoming.

Of course, what I am talking about is like playing three-dimensional chess, infinitely more complex than plain or linear chess. On one hand, I can quickly heal a personal problem if I lift it into the impersonal plane, but if I don't enter the personal plane at all, I can't bridge into unity. At the same time, if I try to deal with a personal problem at the impersonal level, I have lost the integrity of the divine impersonal dimension and the healing won't take place. If I try to personalize the spirit, I end up with a false God or in the clutches of an organization; I create a religion or indulge in spiritual hypocrisy. But because I am a simultaneous being, I can and must simultaneously relate to the problem and still not take it seriously. That's the "double thread."

The Science of Alternatives

My niece and her husband have dedicated most of their lives to what is called "alternative education." At first, I thought that they were just against the public school system, but then I found out that they were dedicated to alternative education for very spiritual reasons. They were not out to resist the evils of public education but rather to offer an alternative.

The difference between the dark forces of totalitarianism which demands conformity and the Christ message is that conformity eliminates the freedom of multiple identities and simultaneity while the Christ spirit offers spontaneity and inclusion.

Everything in Jesus's message honors the individual and offers free choice which is only possible through alternatives. Even the two commandments represent alternative approaches. The "double thread" is the science of alternatives.

In a day when Big Brother computerizes everyone, there is nothing more important than offering alternatives from daily routine. By law, everyone is considered to be alike. By grace, there are no two exactly alike: no two moments, no two situations, no two people. It is impossible to live by spirit rather than law unless there are alternatives from which to choose as inner guidance dictates.

A simple test you can apply to see if any system—educational, governmental, religious, recreational, medical or social—is spiritual is to see if that system offers alternatives. Without alternatives, the multi-dimensional self is locked into a controlled state, controlled either by another person or a system, and the system becomes the end rather than the means. Guilt is born when alternatives are denied and the law of morality is the result.

I have this passion for eliminating morality. Hypocritical present-day morality is humankind's way of hating. Anything that makes people feel guilty is a form of hate and morality engenders and deifies guilt.

Oh sure, morality as designed for a good purpose. It keeps people from making mistakes but by not offering alternatives and by not realizing the necessity of making mistakes in order to learn and be creative, we push people into violating this man-made code of morality. Instead of helping the individual improve, morality brings on self-hate. Morality should be a positive study of how to choose the right alternative, not a negative system of self-denial.

Because God is the only power, our shortcomings are lessons which teach us when we have chosen the wrong alternative. Because there are alternatives, we can be led to the right one. Because grace is the process of truth, alternatives are the offsprings of grace. To me, a moral person is one who has the integrity to choose the right alternatives.

Integrity

Integrity depends on our choice of alternatives. Integrity is tied right in with multi-dimensional being and simultaneity. What may be either integrity or sin for one person may not be for another.

It took a long lecture tour to make me realize how I was violating my integrity. After months of lecturing, I had to retrench and stop all talking for a while. I saw I had lost my integrity because I lost balance through too much talking and writing. I needed to retreat.

I was so tired of hearing people talk about God and spirit all the time that I wanted to scream at the mention of anything to do with the spiritual life. Because I wrote books about spiritual subjects, many believed that when they told me about their own special brand of spiritual baloney, I was supposed to agree. It was all I could do to keep from abusing their sacred cows on the spot. I had lost my integrity, not because I wanted to scream but because I had gotten out of balance by choking off my own alternatives. I wasn't being the "double thread." I was too heavily loaded at the spiritual dimension and my humanity was aching to be heard.

After a couple of years of solitude and quietness, once more I felt something was missing. I meditated and the voice said that the pendulum had swung too far to the other side. Instead of giving too much, I now wasn't giving enough. I hadn't learned to alternate. Balance is a matter of integrity. In fact, balance is spiritual morality. A tight-rope walker alternately leans to one side and then the other to stay on the straight and narrow.

A forty-watt light bulb has integrity if that bulb lights a closet. A hundred-watt bulb has integrity if it lights my living room. It isn't integrity to put the hundred-watt bulb in the closet. It's overkill. And it isn't integrity to try to light the living room with a forty-watt bulb. It's underkill.

If you are a thousand-watt bulb, your light should be a public offering to a whole neighborhood. It would not be integrity for you to be falsely modest in a closet. By the same token, there are many forty-watt bulbs who lay their teacher trips on all and sundry, trying to act like thousand-watt bulbs which they are not. That, too, reveals a lack of integrity, a violation of spiritual morality.

A sense of simultaneity and the integrity of alternatives make us aware of all the potential dimensions which are existing within us and yet keep us realistic about the level from which we are to operate at the moment. If we choose, we can consciously exercise alternatives and save ourselves a lot of trouble.

Simultaneity and Grace

Jesus showed us how we can have the integrity to be consciously both wave and particle simultaneously and alternatively, how we can indeed be aware of the wave as the particle. The Christ's message is about the cause and solution to our problems through an understanding of simultaneity because simultaneity is *Grace*, or rather grace is simultaneity. Simultaneity loves every level, even the level of illusion, of particle as well as of wave because it is all inclusive.

Simultaneity says that though we have "individually" evolved from an embryo into an ever-growing child, into maturity, and then beyond, we are not limited to the law of one or the other. Simultaneously, we are all levels now. (Have you ever met a saint who wasn't simultaneously childlike?) Through our thinking level, we may have comprehended our stages of being in terms of the human time continuum but that's a limitation we can now transcend—through mantra and meditation into simultaneity.

The "double thread" is based precisely on the denial of any finite being as a single or absolute presence by proclaiming a simultaneous creation where past and future are combined.

Just as a seed potentially has within it not only the fully grown plant but even the plant's fruit, we have within us all we will ever be. By grace we are both single and multi-dimensional simultaneously. And, what's more, we don't have to withdraw (in fact, we must not withdraw). We must not believe that there is a state more superior than the frustrating one we presently comprehend, nor that there is any level to which we do not have access at the same time.

Except for certain significant individuals such as Jesus or Buddha, who were in advance of the collective evolution, a conscious realization of simultaneity has been unattainable. Not now. Just knowing about it frees you to experience it. That is why we can thrill at everything around us, at every level of awareness, at both being and not being. Of self and no-self.

I've always said, "The kingdom of Heaven is either right here, right now, or it never was and never will be." Well, it is here now because multi-dimensional awareness, multi-dimensional being, is right here. Grace is the cause and Heaven is the experience of that reality.

How does that apply to me personally, to my particle level? Simply, both when I wink at my own identity or when I encounter the child dimension of myself or in anyone of any age, I can be aware that all levels are in the seed simultanously. I can refuse to limit. I can "I-dentify"—acknowledge it as part of myself.

FIVE

The New Brain

Courage! One more piece of the puzzle. A most important one, the movement into the new brain. No matter how exquisitely many-leveled and simultaneous we are, if we can't communicate with God, the source, we continue to miss the boat. The reason we can't close the gap is because there really isn't any gap. If we can't communicate with God, it's because, despite all the talk, we still believe God is somewhere outside of ourselves. We communicate by using our brains, and until we quite literally, even physically, find the brain of God within our own heads, we can't communicate.

The evolution of that actual God brain within humankind didn't take place overnight. Each gland or organ in our bodies took centuries, if not eons, developing until it reached current sophistication. If we were to outline the stages of physical evolution from the first simple one-cell amoeba to complicated human form, the appearance of human beings would mark the stage at which the rational thinking mind had come into being. Other animals think but they don't know they think; they don't rationalize.

The advent of *homo sapiens* on earth represents the advent of the embodiment of the rational mind. I suspect that humankind's development would parallel the stages the human mind goes through until its final maturity and its proper use. I don't know what the next form of life beyond humankind would be, probably angels. Anyway, as our minds increased in power and flexibility, so did our creative powers and our dominance over the earth.

It's interesting that the seven stages of development of the mind parallel the seven concepts of God which human beings have believed in. First, people believed that Gods were material things on which they depended for survival and they worshipped those things such as the sun and fire. Second, they associated those earth elements with human personalities and names, such as Zeus. Third, they believed that the Gods took human forms which appeared on earth such as the Pharaohs. Fourth, they believed that there were humans who had special access to God's power, such as the priests and shamans. Fifth, they believed that God was actually within certain ordinary individuals, such as the saints. Sixth, that God was potentially in all humans, a belief which has come into acceptance more recently. And now, seventh, we are beginning to realize that God literally dwells right within everyone's head, in the third eye, that God is embodied as the human brain.

We have all been through most of these stages. I had one such experience that I am hesitant to tell about but as it was a step in my own evolution and as telling it may help others consciously close the gap and realize that God is within them too, I will.

The two most shocking experiences anyone can have in life are, first, the shock they experience when they actually see God as another person, and the second is when they experience God as themselves. It seems you can't have the second without the first.

You might say that my experience was similar to that which many chelas (Hindu for "disciples") have with their gurus. Most Hindu teachers claim that it is necessary for one to see one's guru as God on earth in order to surrender one's ego.

Well, I had seen Joel heal people in almost Jesus-like miraculous ways. I had meditated with him before he went on the platform where he claimed to have nothing to say, but from the moment he opened his mouth, extraordinary truths poured forth in eloquent language.

On one of my earlier visits to Hawaii, where Joel lived, it came to me during meditation that the Christ is always embodied somewhere and maybe He was Joel. I was stunned and even scared of the thought. It certainly didn't fit the sophisticated producer image I was wearing at the time. Nevertheless, I told Joel what I had seen and he either didn't hear me or wisely shrugged it off as being a stage in my own evolution where I was able to see spirit embodied. The ability to see God personalized became the link within me to the possibility of experiencing my own divinity in physical terms. Just how this could be revealed itself through an idea which came to me in Key West years later.

After these early experiences in Hawaii, I had a number of changes in life styles and home bases. I stopped producing plays in New York and took up permanent residence in Key West where I already had a winter home. With nothing better to do and needing to keep creative, I bought an old, dilapidated building which had been the first bank on the island and restored it. Needing to fill the building up, I got the idea of starting a hand print fabric printing company, Key West Hand Prints, which ended up having outlets all across the country.

When I sold my interest in the factory, I moved from Key West in order to keep from crystallizing, but I still owned the building there. The factory outgrew the building and had to move; so I had to return to Key West for a while to supervise renovations, like it or not.

Like it, I didn't. The masks of identity which I had inhabited when I lived there some fifteen years before didn't fit me any longer, so rather than socializing I spent my time working on the building all day and I spent my evenings pretty much alone, semifrustrated. Perhaps I had to be stuck in Key West and feel exasperated in order to be pushed into meditating deeply enough to create the internal climate suitable for this God revelation to break through.

Well, one night I was half reading a book which wasn't holding my attention any too well while half listening to the public TV channel with equal non-attention. A University of Miami psychologist was being interviewed about the functions of the human brain. Sounded dull but I was too lazy to get up and change the channel; so I kept on half listening. His expertise was the physiological or biological explanation of brain functions and he was repeating the stuff we've all heard so much these past years.

At one point, he held up a plastic model of the brain. He removed the right lobe and then the left lobe, and explained the operation of each of the lobes. He claimed that biologists had proven that there were certain spots in the left brain which controlled the right side of the body, that there were certain memory banks in each lobe, and that we now know where those memory banks are and can go in and operate and change the way one responds, and so on and on.

I'll repeat some of what he said because it is significant groundwork for what followed. The left brain is the masculine brain, it is the logical brain. It is the "A, therefore *B*, therefore *C*, and we arrive at *D*" rational side. That is the thrust side, the aggressive side. It's the side we have always honored in our society. We favor that brain. It's a Western world brain. It's the neighbor side of the brain.

The right brain is the feminine brain. It's the intuitive side, the emotional side, the instinctive as opposed to the rational. It's the spiritual side. Well, neither of these brains trusts the other. The logical brain cannot understand the intuitive brain and vice versa. Both are necessary. They are complements of each other and we all have both lobes but neither of them is really spiritual as such, because each of the lobes relates to phenomena. These lobes are storage batteries. So, having been overloaded with theories about the right and left lobes, I continued to split my attention.

All of a sudden, I heard the psychologist say something that shot me to attention. I dropped my book all ears. He didn't know what he was really saying. Well, at least not the spiritual implications, but though he was only discussing the subject of the evolution of the brain from a physiological approach, it set a chain of realizations bursting through my mind. Here was the missing link between God and man, the link that put God physically inside of mankind.

He said, "The exciting thing at the forefront of our study of the brain is the discovery of the new brain." He went on, "You see, we know we have these two big lobes but in between is a ganglia of glands, the pituitary, the hypothalamus, and the pineal. We know that these glands regulate everything else in the body." He said they knew what these glands did but didn't yet know how they did it. These glands, according to the psychologist, should be considered a kind of brain because they had such an effect on our conduct and bodies, particularly the pineal gland.

Take the pineal. The scientists know what the pineal does, though again not how. They know that this one gland affects or regulates all the other glands in some remarkable ways. It has the power to signal other glands and other parts of the body to function in different ways. For instance, the pineal controls the secretion of testosterone and estrogen, male and female hormones.

Scientists tell us there is a "homeo box" master gene in the body from which evolves all the hundreds of thousands of other genes which, in turn, form the body. They say that there is a protein which makes these genes communicate and it probably comes from the pineal. At least, the pineal is the control system. Apparently the pineal is our communication center uniting all the functions of the body.

Medical scientists have just announced that these glands are responsible for instigating all the healing process in the body. Among many other diverse functions, the pineal produces endorphins.

Endorphins are nature's pain killers, nature's tranquilizers, nature's pacifiers, nature's drugs if you will. Ordinarily we are not aware that we are constantly supplied with this delicious blessing. Some people are even naturally endowed with more endorphins than others and live in a state of euphoria. In fact, we lock some people up and call them insane because they are so blissfully intoxicated by runaway endorphins.

If the divine process of life didn't supply endorphins, women couldn't have babies. As a pregnant woman gets closer and closer to giving birth, more and more endorphins are secreted within her. She could not possibly stand the pain of the birthing experience without them. When we see the mother-to-be, everyone says, "Doesn't she look beautiful. She looks absolutely radiant." It's because she's stoned.

By the same token, if the divine process hadn't filled babies with endorphins, those tender little bodies couldn't possibly stand the pain of being squeezed through the birth canal out into the world. Notice how babies flop around like little drunk men? They're drugged, but God's the druggist.

It's also why the Hindu saint, Ramakrishna was called "the God-intoxicated man." He was so full of endorphins from meditating that he appeared drunk. Meditation affects the pineal gland and causes a greater secretion of endorphins. You may have noticed that the Brahman class of Hindus, the spiritual cast, paint the red dot right in front of the pineal gland. That's why they call it the third eye, it sees beyond the duality of the other two. That's no accident. Mystics have known for thousands of years that there is some connection between this spot in one's head and one's spiritual life.

My Own Addiction

Before I get off the subject of the endorphins to speculate on the function of pineal gland itself, let me explain why an alcoholic or drug addict's having to stop "cold turkey" is so much worse than any of us who haven't experienced it can ever imagine. You see, the desire to get drunk or to take drugs is the desire to bring on and intensify artificially the experience that the pineal produces naturally, or the desire to have by choice what one can have access to naturally if the conditions are right. The addict's problem is that anything one rejects, anything one denies for a long enough time eventually stops functioning. If people seek their endorphin experiences artificially through a drink or a drug, the pineal eventually stops supplying endorphins; it's been rejected.

So when an addict stops cold turkey, he or she no longer gets endorphins in the natural way as the rest of us do and he or she isn't getting them artificially either. He or she is in Hell until the natural flow starts again. If you want to know what Hell is, that is it. We who have always had a natural supply can't possibly imagine what it is to burn in that Hell. To be cut off from the pineal is to be cut off from God, to be completely Godless, for the pineal is the source of or directly related to our God contact.

Wait a minute—I have personally experienced that Hell, too. When I had my dark night, when I couldn't make contact in meditation for months and months, I was in Hell. Sure, I know being cut off had a purpose, it was opening me up because the time had come for me to stop blocking the natural flow of—of what?— the new mind.

This is the day of the new mind, the new brain. This is the day we will start living by the new mind. This is the day the new mind will regulate the lower mind where good and bad exist. I had to discover what was blocking my next step. (I'll deal with it in the very next chapter.)

I can assure you first hand, after years of meditating, that, when I make contact, I feel this warmth come over me. I feel it smooth out my very body like a divine tranquilizer. The result is very real. I can't always make that contact happen when I want it to, but when it does, I know it and I feel it both mentally and physically. I'm a spiritual addict. I'm hooked. I'm hooked on what takes place if and when I can enter that silence which somehow affects the flow of natural endorphins. I can get by for a day or two without this prayerful experience but, like an addicts who needs his fix, before long I am climbing a wall if I can't achieve what I call my "God contact." But the point is that the physical as well as the spiritual faculty is right within my own body.

Long after I have made my contact and as long as I can renew it, I feel the warmth of that presence, that peace. Paradoxically you can't have that experience without contemplating the mind of God. Perhaps that is what the Scripture meant when it said, "Thou will keep him in perfect peace, whose *mind* is stayed on Thee."

It's the same with most of you. You know that. When you go out and see a beautiful sunset, you sit there and you drop all thought and feel this wonderful peace settle on you. It's not accidental. You've made some inner contact, some love of life, that has made your pineal active. It is now giving you this wonderful experience of God's love. Ah, that's what love is, too. Now we're bringing love down and relating it to a chemical substance. What is that telling us? It is telling us that we have that spirit materially within us.

It's not speculation any longer. This is no spiritual mumbo jumbo. I'm talking about something real, something you can put your hand on. You don't have to be airy fairy about this. This is material. Science has proved it. There is a relationship between the experience of God or love and a very physical function in our bodies.

Let me explain. Naturally I'm not saying that God is just a material gland, but there is a practical metaphysical principle for locating the spiritual center in physical form. All consciousness expresses itself in form. Form is just a different dimension of consciousness. There's always a form that represents a function. That, too, is what the two commandments stand for. In other words, God expressed in form is neighbor, man and woman. Human beings are God embodied. Well then, if all consciousness is expressed in form, it is localized and materially represented, and if the pineal represents the qualities of God, then it is the seat of God within us. If we want to find a presence of God within us, it's the pineal, third eye.

The Presence of God

We've just now come to realize how important the different gland centers are. Long ago Edgar Cayce in one of his readings noted that the seven gland centers represent the seven positions of the kundalini. You might even parallel these with the seven evolving concepts of God I mentioned earlier. When we meditate and pass through or contact these centers, we are moving through gland centers. Each time we do, our lives are affected at different levels. So, the pineal obviously represents the highest spiritual center and there is some tie between it and the spirit. We are a universe within ourselves and all the universe is represented somewhere within us. God is represented as the new brain.

All right, so mankind has been developing the new brain for a few thousand years and now, at last, the new mind has developed to the point where we can consciously recognize and live by it. When we can, the spiritual life will no longer be the pubescent fantasy it has been. At last it is functioning in its full glory and we don't have to look outside for all the qualities of God. They are within us.

If we have a pineal, we have God's entry way. The gland is his evidence and location. If we understand the function of the pineal, we may understand how God works. But more than that, anything which can bring us a step closer to experiencing God *not* outside of ourselves is important.

By studying or understanding the consciousness or function of the pineal gland, we may have a clue as to how God works in us as human beings. Like the wave and the particle, you can't understand the new mind in terms of the old mind. The old two-lobed mind is the particle mind, personal sense, but the new mind is impersonal. The right- and left-lobed minds are like a data bank filled with bits of information. The left lobe of the old-mind computer is filled with intellectual knowledge and the right side is filled with intuitive knowledge. The left is the conscious top of the iceberg and the right is the unconscious. You might say that the right and left lobes, the lower brain and the new brain correspond to the two commandments. While the lower brain is the personal neighbor level, the new brain is the impersonal divine level.

The key to understanding the new brain, the pineal, is that it functions impersonally. That is why we can't understand it in a personal way. Its knowledge is judgless, unlike that of the lower mind. The pineal does not react to time. Its impersonal actions are instantaneous, simultaneous, and now. Anyone who lives from the guidance of the pineal observes life impersonally, sees the unity of all life, is beyond fear or judgment. The new brain indeed acts, functions, and manifests a super kind of knowledge, but that knowledge is abstract knowledge and can't be understood by the lower personal sense mind. In other words, it is God's function.

New Mind Scripture

Now really listen to this. Dare to take this trip with me. Dare to get rid of the old wine. Dare to take this step and believe it. I know I am asking you to use your own lower mind to understand the new mind and it can't really do it but listen to some of the Scripture and see if you can't feel this truth.

When Paul said: "I live yet not I, but Christ liveth in me," what do you think he is talking about? He was saying "I live; but not I, this new kind of mind that Jesus had, this Christ mind, lives my life." When he said, "Let this mind be in you which was also in Christ Jesus," what do you think that meant? Obviously he didn't mean to cut Jesus's brain out and implant it physically in your head. The mind he was talking about was the one Jesus lived after he was Christed. That was when He took His orders from the impersonal new mind. He represented the first person in our culture who was able to actually live out of this impersonal

Christ mind. That was the impersonal mind of unconditional love.

What, as the poet Browning said of God, can be "closer than breathing nearer than hands and feet"? The new mind, which is within anyone who has a pineal gland. What else can be closer? What else is inside of us? When we hear that "the Father is within," obviously a tiny man is not running around within us, but the fathering, regulating, directing pineal is.

When Jesus said, "Neither in this mountain nor yet at Jerusalem," He told us not to seek in a building or place but to go within ourselves. Well, what's within? The new mind, His mind, the same mind that was directing Him. Within is the mind of God, the new mind. It is not off somewhere out there. No one can keep it from you. It shines on the saints and the sinners alike. No, more than that, it lives *in* saints and sinners alike. We all have it. It's not out there. We may not use it or know it but we all have it. It is there just waiting to be released. It is available to any of us. We don't have to go anywhere for it.

"I will lift up mine eyes," lift up my consciousness to the third eye, the new mind. "I, if I be lifted up from the earth, will draw all men unto me" means "I, if I be lifted up into my new mind, will draw all men into theirs." If I lift *up* my focus into the new mind, I will draw others into this being.

When I first experienced the meaning of the advent of the new mind, it shook me to the roots because I saw that this concept can wake us out of centuries of darkness where God has been thought of as something apart from us. It puts God right inside us.

Meditation has been the best avenue of developing exercise to shut the lower mind off so we can let this mind that was in Christ Jesus flow. When I began to look into this phenomenon, I began to analyze the functions of the lower mind, the personal mind. It was obvious that the lower mind is what Adam lived by. He ate of the tree of the lower mind, good and bad, masculine and feminine, right and left lobe, duality. That's the personal mind. The lower mind is personal. The new mind is impersonal.

Everyone reading this book has a lower mind. And, what's more important, each one is programmed a bit differently. There are no two exactly alike, just as there are no two computers programmed just alike. There is an infinite variety. But everyone's new mind is the same because the new mind is the universal, impersonal, divine mind. In computer language, it is the DOS. Whether we can open ourselves consciously to it is another matter but we all have it. It's the mind of God. And "where two or three are gathered together in my name," in the new mind, "I will be there."

There are all kinds of religions which find God in the heart. They tell you to focus on the heart, meditate on the heart. For years, I tried to do that but every time I got to the heart center, I felt emotion, I felt passions, longings, I felt lower mind things. That's not bad. I'm not putting them down. They belong to the neighbor level. The heart is the complement of the head. But the lower mind needs the direction of the new mind. Basically, when I sit to meditate, I go zip right up into the third eye, to this space between my eyes. It's that vacuum I seek to arrive at. Just accepting the new mind there is a great help.

To Walk With God

To walk with God means to companion with the new mind. To recognize your sonship is to recognize that your actions are fathered by the new mind. The statement, "I have come that they might have life and that they might have it more abundantly" is the new mind announcing its function in your life.

Masters are simply those who have learned to live by the new mind. We call them "illuminated" because where there was darkness of vision, now there is light. Jesus was such a shining revelation of the new mind that we called Him God.

In dissecting the pineal gland, the scientists find that it glows in the dark. Light as illumination is its nature. That's why you may have noticed that all the old pictures of Jesus and the saints surround their heads with halos. That's no accident. Saints are those who have died to the lower mind and are living out of the new mind, the white light mind. Literally living by the new mind.

The Holy Instant, of which *The Course in Miracles* talks, refers to the instant the new mind is experienced. Once that happens, the love of God is no longer a vague wish. It is recognizable as a result of the new mind of experience.

Now when we seek guidance, we are no longer seeking guidance from anything apart from ourselves. What we are doing is seeking guidance from our new mind. The mind that is there, right in our own skull. When we say that we need guidance, we must realize that we can't enter the new mind with fear, frustrations, or emotions. Those are lower mind expressions. If we want to experience the new mind, we must drop lower thought, and enter the silence where the new mind operates.

When people think they need guides from the other side, what they really want is contact with the universal new mind, but they have been tricked into looking to other sources than their own. They don't need to, once they can experience their own new mind. By seeking guidance through our own new mind, there isn't the danger of the guilt trip or separation we encounter by thinking guidance is coming from something apart from ourselves.

We talk about living by God's will; what is God's will? We say, "Not by my will but thine, Lord." What we really mean is "not my lower mind will but thine, the new mind." The new mind's will is what you want to live by. God's will is your will. It is right there within you. There is no unformed consciousness, as I said. Christ is always embodied. God is embodied in you. God's will is embodied in your will. We talk about the "divine mind." The divine mind is the new mind.

SIX

The Primal Problem

It is wonderful to discover we have God within us but, if we can't communicate with that part of us, we might as well not have it. After we get a sense of the beautiful complexity of our identities, each of us has to discover what has been blocking the free flow of communications within the community of himself. There is only one obstacle to all communications but it takes many forms. Before I pinpoint the central problem, I want to explain the particular result of this one cause and the form it took in my own life.

Until I was about thirty-seven years old, I was really fortunate. There were at least a few people with whom I could communicate holistically. I had my mother, van Druten, Goldsmith, and Prabvananda; all of them, I might add, were considerably older than I. But when the time came for me to come out from under the influence of parental figures or gurus, I ran smack up against the problem of loneliness.

Loneliness

I had already broken all the laws of lack and limitation in the material world. I knew how, through the power of imagery or consciousness, to communicate with or manifest supply. Money, success, and acclaim came from every direction. I was also able to heal others by spiritual communication and even to heal myself. But instead of death being my last enemy, a feeling of loneliness was. From that time until I had an experience at fifty-four (which I will relate when we get to the cause of my loneliness), I continued to feel separate; never seemed to fit completely in anywhere or to have an in-depth, one-to-one relationship with another person.

Oh, I was gregarious enough. I put on a good face, played the game, had a number of acquaintances I called good friends, had some minor sexual affairs, but inside I felt that I was faking sociability and that something was wrong with me. I wasn't fully communicating with others or with myself. Something was blocking me. Sure, I knew how to talk but not how to communicate holistically. In fact, I talked all the time, hoping I could communicate by talking and hang on to others that way. The lonelier I felt, the more I talked and the more I talked, the lonelier I became.

Loneliness also applied to every problem or anxiety I have ever had. When I say "loneliness," I'm not just talking about being alone. You can be surrounded by people and still feel lonely. Loneliness doesn't just have to do with other people. Ultimately, any time there is a feeling of rejection or a sense of separation, it's a form of loneliness.

When I talk about loneliness, I am talking about the feeling of being rejected or disconnected not only from other people but also from life or from God. If you really examine it, every fear you have ever had has been a manifestation of loneliness, separation, or rejection.

Look at it this way. There is only one sin, a sense of separation from God. It takes many different forms, like an actor who wears many different masks, but the only cause of all sin is the belief in a life apart from God.

The fear of rejection or loneliness is humankind's "primal fear." We have been taught that the primal motivation of human nature is based on survival, that the fear of death is the primal fear. But it isn't; otherwise people would not sacrifice their lives for others, they would not go to war, or even commit suicide. People commit suicide in the hope of ending their feeling of isolation and separation, in order to live, not to die.

Death is feared not because we fear leaving this world but because we fear being separated from loved ones and experiencing the unknown alone. Our fear of losing our loved ones has nothing to do with them, as such. It is our fear of being lonely, of being separated.

I realized when my own mother died that I wasn't mourning her passing. Her going was neat; she wrapped up life, didn't have to suffer illness, and was ready. I knew she had life eternal. What I was mourning was my own separation. I felt rejected. In fact, part of me was even angry at her for rejecting me, for leaving me behind.

In material terms, rejection by our mothers is the most devastating human experience we can have. That's why we are so desperate to constantly have their approval. We fear being rejected from the womb of God out of which we came.

All our so-called sins are misdirected attempts to eliminate loneliness. For instance, if people rob a bank, it is because they believe money will help them communicate. It will buy them companionship or the things that will keep them from being separated. They want to be rich because they feel that if they have enough possessions, they won't be separated from life.

Why is loneliness the prime fear? Because somewhere we know the truth—that we live and move and have our being in God. That means we know we are one with infinity, that we are not separate finite beings. As long as we can stay in touch with and communicate with life or God, we are safe. When that awareness is within one of us, even sub-consciously, he or she is not "cast forth as a branch and is withered." But when he or she feels cut off from God, he or she is life-less.

Every form of life depends on the totality of all that exists or ever came into existence. The more we become consciously aware of our interrelationship with all being, the freer we become because we are freed from the illusion of separateness and are able to experience ourselves as true centers of being, free of primal fear.

All of our other fears are secondary fears. Fear of lack, fear of incapacity, fear of disgrace—these are all facets of a single primal fear. The fear of being rejected by God is behind all other feelings of loneliness. Even what we ordinarily think of as loneliness is brought on simply because we do not know how to communicate with God and therefore ourselves.

At the time my loneliness was most intense, a friend wrote to me, "In your aloneness is your allness." I didn't want to hear that because I was confusing "loneliness" with "aloneness." Aloneness is just what the word says, "all-one-ness." All oneness is perfect communication and sometimes we have to feel loneliness in order to be pushed into oneness, into God.

Ever since I made that first meditative communication with God, I pray or meditate whenever I am lonely or fearful. When I am able to communicate with God's presence successfully, the loneliness goes away. It isn't that successful prayer heals the fear. Once communication is established, the illusion of separation dissolves itself.

When you realize, "I am not alone. The Father and I are one," fear has to leave. Its cause is removed. When we try to find a material solution to any problem, it is like putting salve on the sore rather than removing the cause. The problem is a sense of separation which has led to a lack of communications. Until we establish our communication with God, the primal fear continues to exist. Remove the cause and we won't need any more salve.

By the same token, the belief in a personal savior or guru is of very real importance to many people. Though people can't see their particular Jesus or guru with their eyes, they don't feel alone if they believe in his presence. It isn't that Jesus takes fear away from them. They no longer fear because the primal fear of loneliness isn't present if they feel their Saviour's presence. They are communicating with their guru. As long as there is a communication with infinity, the fear of loneliness can be kept at bay. Whenever people talk of "oneness," they are talking of the opposite of separation and the solution to the primal fear.

Listening

Surprisingly, listening is the key to communication, not talking. My own loneliness finally went away when I began to learn how to listen. Listening is still a problem but I'm better at it now and no longer lonely.

We have to shut up in order to communicate. The most potent healing power psychologists and spiritual counselors have is their ability to listen. The words they speak to their patients may help a bit but by carefully listening to their patients, they eliminate the primal fear. By being listened to, the patient no longer feels alone and is healed of the fear of separation. The patient is healed by the spiritual power of listening. It is a spiritual matter. The spirit of listening and caring has established communication and dissolved loneliness.

The patient no longer feels alone and separated because the therapist has listened, and after the fear has abated, the patient is then open, free, and able to hear words of truth from the therapist because truth follows oneness. Or I should say, "the fact that there is no separation *is* the truth."

The most important aspect of listening is that when we are listened to by someone whom we value and respect, our being listened to gives us permission to listen to ourselves, and that is what it is all about: self-love.

Perhaps the value of seminars or retreats is that they provide communication experiences which give greater reinforcements to "you are not alone" and pacify the primal fear. Perhaps they provide time for people to listen to each other in greater depth, for love is the supreme communication.

Ask yourself who it is in your life you love the most. You will find it is those who listen to you, those who communicate with you, those who make you feel less alone, those who have the capacity to know you and communicate with you. They are the bridges between you and God and you love them for that.

Listening is the secret of communication. Remember—you can't hear God if you don't listen. There is one thing that blocks our ability to listen to ourselves, to others, or to God. It is the same stumbling block, the number one obstacle to all communication, the one which keeps us from realizing that Heaven is here and now: personal sense.

The Paradox of Personal Sense

I was fifty-four before I finally recognized what really caused my loneliness and was blocking my way to Heaven. It's suprising how one can be advanced in some ways and be blind in others. I was always ahead in the esoteric, spiritual dimensions but lagging at the personal level. I had travelled the world, experienced Zen, Tibetan, and Hindu ashrams, associated with the most significant metaphysicians of the age, and lectured to thousands; I was an accomplished spiritual healer, and had even written several successful books. But I felt like someone who had received several doctoral degrees in higher math who had found out he didn't know how to add.

You might wonder how I could write truth-full books without having arrived myself, but I couldn't write at all unless and until I "heard" what to write. In order to write, I would have to go away somewhere by myself, go through a kind of death process until I would get out of my way and begin to hear. Because I type quickly, I could just write down what I heard from the inner voice. To write from guidance, I needed a capacity to listen but not necessarily to have attained the consciousness of what I had heard. If I were to rewrite those books today, I'd only make minor changes and none to do with the principles I wrote about.

I didn't realize then that people shouldn't put into print principles they are not prepared to live because the seed is planted in consciousness and sooner or later they are going to have to live them. I did.

It didn't help either, when I read Gurdjieff who said that if one hadn't broken through the "fifth center," the mental center where truth is intellectually understood, into the spiritual center by the time one was forty that it was too late to attain the actual experience. He was saying that the new brain couldn't be activated after forty except in cases of great violence. Either he was wrong, or the dark night I experienced was just that: a spiritual violence powerful enough to blast me through.

My dark night had begun several years before.

Thank God, this did more than anything else in my life to collapse my overblown inflation, that distance between what I knew with my new mind and what I could communicate to myself or others. There were a few respites of light during the spiritual eclipse and with each one I would tell myself that the dark was over but until it had served its purpose, the dark night returned from time to time.

If I was asked to pick out a specific date when I first recognized not only the beginning of this dark night process but what it was ultimately destined to bring on, it would be the moment I read, *The Spiritual Journey of Joel S. Goldsmith*. Joel had passed on some nine years before and Harper & Row had just printed his biography. They were also my publisher and were then producing one of my books, the last before this one. I stopped in New York to see them on my way to Virginia Beach where I was to be the featured speaker at the Edgar Cayce Foundation's Easter seminar. The publisher gave me an advance copy of Joel's book. My guidance told me not to read it until after Easter as something in it might disturb me and affect my Easter message. My guidance also said that I wouldn't fully know the significance of what I read until the sixth of May.

After Easter, I began to read the book. Near the end of it was a letter Joel had written to his editor, Loraine Sinkler, from London some six months before he died. Having known Joel as intimately as I had for over eighteen years, the letter shook me to my roots. It was a letter describing the dark night he was currently in himself, written in heart-wrenching tearful words.

I wanted to throw the book across the room. If that was what Joel was feeling just before he died and that was what I was feeling at the moment, my only thought was, "Is this what I get for having studied your work for all these years? Is that how I will end up?"

Sure enough, it wasn't until I was trying to meditate my way out of my depression on the morning of the sixth of May that the answer came. At the very end of Joel's letter, he had written, "So I guess I have another notch higher to go. This is all such a new experience for me." There it was. His dark night had been a necessary initiation needed to push him into further growth, "another notch higher to go." Something in his own development was yet missing. There was nothing wrong with his teaching, not a bit, it was perfect mysticism, but something needed to be added.

The next clue was in his words, "This is all such a new experience for me." It was. Joel lived almost all the time in and with an awareness of his spiritual dimension. During his dark night, he was stuck solely at the human or personal level and that was a shock to him. He didn't know how to accept or handle his humanity.

You see, most people spend their whole lives finding out how to experience their divinity, not just to think of it but actually to experience it. In reverse, some people go through a great deal of their life never experiencing, understanding, nor facing their humanity. Spiritual contact or freedom from the kind of problems that plague most of society doesn't seem to be a problem to them, but when it comes to pragmatic reality, they are at a loss.

Experiencing one's divinity isn't a moral issue, not even what we ordinarily think of as a spiritual issue. It simply means that some people find it easier to be free of being earth bound than others, can break the laws of human nature, aren't tempted to accept limitation, and value invisibles more than visibles.

Joel and I were among those. As a child, I was always singing, fantasizing, and living in a world where I thought anything was possible. Dick Tracy was my hero. Throughout my life, my mother use to say, "Living around Walter is amazing. There's always a parking space, success comes through the air, anything can happen." Even when I was producing plays, I didn't know that I couldn't be successful without bribing the union or the box office. When people stuck their hands out, I just shook them and somehow my innocence broke that unwritten law and I got away with it.

I thought I was like everyone else. I did everything everyone else did. I drank. I had sex. I hustled life. But I didn't realize that from either a past life experience or because I was born with certain instinctive metaphysical awareness, I could break the law of limitation. By that I mean that human nature sets up laws of health, laws of lack, and laws of impossibility, and I was able to set those aside. Not through religion necessarily but through image initiation, positive thinking, and spirit, I could manipulate the human scene.

Again everything I had learned before, not only from Joel but many fine teachers and teachings, were all necessary. They were the foundation on which I had built but something was blocking me. The double thread was my tool but something was stalling its use.

It was almost two years to the day from the time my dark night started before the missing piece fell into place. During the first year of that time, I was on a national lecture tour with my new book. Most of the time, I did a masterful job of putting a smiling mask on my desperation and misery. Thousands of names were piling up on my mailing list. People were trying to "guru-ize" me and put me on a pedestal. Fortunately I knew something was missing and wouldn't fake it or found no reason to. I wasn't kidding myself.

Before I hit bottom, I was so desperate that I didn't know which way to turn. My inner guidance had totally cut out on me and I couldn't even decide what can of beans to buy at the grocery store. You see, most of my motivation, as I have stated, was intuitive or the result of inner guidance. By the time I was in my fifties, there wasn't much logical or left-brain ability left. So when guidance cut out, I was desperate. Now for the first time, I knew what it was like to experience the Hell which most people live in all the time, the agony of having to decide with their minds what is right and what is wrong based on survival fears. Without my guidance, life was a nightmare. I just begged God, "Let me go. Let me go." I wanted out.

The one thing that kept me from totally giving up or from contemplating suicide was that, when this dark night had started, my guidance had said that when I reached my fifty-fourth birthday, I would come out of the tunnel and I would have my answer.

I've always been a real believer in the seven year cycles which start when rational thought has evolved in our fifth year. My life has fallen into a definite seven-year pattern. One of these, as Carl Jung explains, is the one that ends at age forty, at which time he claims we get rid of our father figures or our teachers; and our individual life expressions begin. That would mean that fifty-four would be another and significant moment. So I kept on keeping on.

As I approached my fifty-fourth birthday, I settled down in a little house I had purchased in San Antonio in order to somehow keep functioning until the promised breakthrough. I had just been to the Findhorn Community in Scotland where they emphasized the spiritual link between plants and people, and found that the only time I could have a moment of peace was when I worked in my garden. Meditation, my lifeline until then, was a blank, unyielding wall.

A few weeks before my birthday, I had planted some radish seeds in my garden and the day before my birthday, a young friend who lived in the neighborhood was visiting. I pulled up my first ripe radish, washed it off and handed it to him. He looked at it and said, "I'm eating dirt."

At first, I thought he was cuckoo but then I realized what he was implying. He had seen me plant these tiny, almost invisible seeds just a few weeks before, and in that short time, they had transmuted the dirt into this luscious red fruit. Now that's a miracle. When I attempted to meditate at my birthday's dawn, the radish experience of the day before was on my mind.

I thought of the radish. And for the first time in ages, I began to "hear" again. It said, "Walter, you may not be better than the radish but you are as good as the radish. That means the same principle of life, the same miracle that is growing the radish, is growing you." I asked, "Then what's wrong?" and it answered, "You don't fully trust it." I asked, "Why" and it answered, "Because of personal sense."

There it was: "personal sense." Personal sense is the whole ball of wax, so ordinary that we miss it. We keep looking for dramatic, esoteric, new age secrets when, if we solve this one old-fashioned problem, we wouldn't have any others. We would no longer be lonely nor even fear. In order to do so, we have to understand what personal sense means and how it operates before we can make one and one into two. One God and one neighbor (the personal) make the two that is really *one*. Dealing with personal sense is the meat and potatoes of the spiritual meal.

Personal sense is just another way of saying "self-centeredness." I hate to admit it but it took me until I was fifty-four before I realized that the thing which had been blocking me and making me lonely all along was self-centeredness. That's how personal sense is manifest. Like it or not, my inflation, that gap between my spiritual knowledge and capacity to live it, still existed because I had remained self-centered.

My inner dialogue that day went on to say, and this is all important, "Self-centeredness has nothing to do with morality. It is not a spiritual matter. You can be Schweitzer ministering to the pygmies in Africa doing a wonderful world work and still be self-centered. You can write books that help thousands and still be self-centered. Until self-centeredness is conquered, the umbilical cord tying you to this world will not be broken." Self-centeredness or personal sense isn't a spiritual matter because it has nothing to do with your divinity. It is purely a psychological condition of your humanity and, as all of us are born into our humanity, we all have the problem of self-centeredness.

These days when I try to talk to someone about their self-centeredness, I prefer using the words, "self-consciousness" interchangably. "Self-centeredness" still has the onus of good or bad, of our human morality, and lays a guilt trip on others, while "self-consciousness" is really the same thing without the sound of condemnation. We feel compassion for a self-conscious or shy person and should for a self-centered person, because it's the same thing. They are both blocked by a sense of self. I know lots of sweet, dear, and even spiritual-minded people who are helplessly locked in a self-conscious state wondering what is blocking their ability to live by the truths they have found. They don't realize that until they conquer personal sense, they are still tied to the earth. They can study spiritual truths until they are blue in the face but until they conquer personal sense, none of it helps.

By the same token, shy self-conscious "Miss Mouse" in the office is not humble. She's self-centered, probably has the biggest ego in the office.

Any time a person's self-consciousness comes between him and others, between him and life, that person is being blocked by personal sense. To be self-centered really is like viewing the world through colored glasses. Everything is colored by self-awareness.

Self-consciousness is no one's fault. As I said, it is not a moral issue. We are born into self-consciousnes but until we become free of it, we can't see ourselves as multi-dimensional beings and are anchored in limitation. We can't fly. I don't think mine was a critical case of self-centeredness but I had a bad enough case to block my spiritual progress and make me lonely.

I guess a psychologist analyzing my personal life would say that my dear mother added to my self-centeredness. My father died when I was only nine and mother centered her affections on me. I became our favorite subject. She always encouraged me to talk about myself. It wasn't until after she died that I had to deal with my self-centeredness.

I've known many of the world's famous personalities. In almost every case, their fame has been a spiritual curse. The world, as a result of their success, has pushed them into self-centeredness. Everyone talks about them, everyone asks them to speak about themselves, everyone insists that they are what their reputations appear to be. Unless they are blessed by God, the large amounts of money which celebrities are swamped with, because of their gifts to the world, lock them into self-centeredness. That is why it is easier for a camel to pass through the eye of a needle than for a rich man to experience God. Riches crystallize. Any one rich in personality, in talent, in beauty is in danger of self-centeredness.

The Mask

When I looked up the derivation of the words "person" and "personal" in the dictionary, I was surprised at what I found. The word "personal" comes from the Latin word, "persona" which in turn means "mask." When we talk about our persona, we are talking about the mask or the degree of personal sense we are wearing. Our personality is our mask.

In ancient days, actors wore face masks in their performances. Literally, the word "personare," from which "persona" came, is divided into "per" meaning "through" and "sona" meaning "mask." So anything seen or spoken through the mask of self is personal. Or, vice versa, anything of a personal nature is coming out of the mask and may not be reality. Personal sense is anything that is done through the mask or false sense of self. Obviously, if the mask is speaking, communications are not only limited but false. Masks muffle true communications. Masks distort true being. Personal sense distorts true being. Until we can act or speak without personal sense, we are not revealing the truth of ourselves.

Shakespeare was right when he said "All the world's a stage and all the men and women merely players." As long as we are embodied, as long as we possess physical bodies, we have to contend with our masks, our personal sense. On the stage of life, no one ever really sees us. They see our masks. We may not be wearing our masks in our dressing room but the only one who sees us there is that rare person who has the capacity for unconditional love. Masks are conditions. We are fortunate if we have one or two in our life who have the love to see us unconditionally naked.

We have a job to perform or we wouldn't be on this earth stage. But, unfortunately, the longer we play our part, the more difficult it becomes to distinguish between our true identity and our mask.

Don't get me wrong. Masks are blessings if we use them in the right way and don't confuse ourselves with them. Thank God we have them. Masks protect us from evil thought. We can hide behind them when needed. Those public figures, such as Janis Joplin, Judy Garland, and Jimmy Hendricks, who self-destructed did so because they exposed too much of themselves. They stood too naked without the spiritual power or love to support and to back them up. Use your mask, but don't be used by it.

The Riddle of Reincarnation

Most people completely miss the point of reincarnation. First of all, the whole concept of reincarnation is at the psychological level. The minute we start defining and categorizing, we are personalizing and dealing with particles and time, both of which are third-dimension aspects. In order to experience reincarnation, as we know it, we would have to have a linear time sense, time to have been one life and time to be another.

The theory of reincarnation is actually man's attempt to explain what he can't explain. Hold on, it has a value, though. In general, I subscribe to reincarnation because it is as close to cluster timeless reality as my human mind can communicate and if I sense its meaning rather than cogitate upon it, I can leap into the wave. Those who can't buy the concept may be stuck with the limitation of logic.

The main value in tuning in to past lives isn't to perpetuate a present personal sense ego or regress to one you think is more glamorous; quite the opposite is true. Most people try to communicate with their past lives through their current eyes, through their current personal sense. Like actors in a repertory company, they see their past lives as the different parts they have played. It is always their present concept of self playing the parts. They say, "I was once Cleopatra" meaning that their current ego is always there. The "I" they talk of is their present personal sense. That would be like Hamlet saying, "Last week I was Macbeth." Hamlet is a fiction and so is Macbeth.

If we think that the main value of reexperiencing past lives is to help us to better cope with our current identities in the present life, we've missed the boat.

We are stuck in a psychological interpretation of life, not a mystical one. The Gita, from which the theory of reincarnation sprang, points out clearly that we do have these incarnations in order to grow, which is psychological, but we have never been any of them because we are not masks but the actor behind the mask. We are the Atman—the inner-most essence—not the incarnation.

Properly understood and experienced, reincarnation can be a great blessing not because it helps you communicate and understand your current human identity but because it can free you from personal sense itself, free you from your present human sense, good or bad. If you can experience past lives, it can help you realize that your current one is no more real and final than those. All those past lives were aspects of personal sense, masks. They all experienced joys and pains, ups and downs, and finally died, but something called "you" (or "I") continued. What was that?

Your present personality or self-concept is as much a fiction as those past ones. Like the actor, it is a part you are playing in this production. But it is a fictional image of your true identity, not anything that will remain or continue after this production ends. You will go on but it won't. If, however, reincarnation can help you experience who you really are, the one which does live on into eternity, you are truly blessed.

First of all, when you realize your true self, you will see that success and failure, happiness and unhappiness, abundance or lack have to do with the character you are performing in the stage play, just as Hamlet's lamentations have nothing to do with the actor who is playing the part. None of those touch the true you. If they did affect you, then you would have died when the character in the drama died and there would be no reincarnation, nothing to reincarnate. So this realization can help you drop your present concerns, see your present life as a part you are playing, free you from being tied to a personal sense of self, and let you communicate who you really are.

Breaking Up the Crust

Like masks, we are always either putting on personal sense or taking it off. I go through a dark night and it breaks up the crust. When that happens, I am free of personal sense, I can let the light shine and I become a creative vehicle. Once I have created something new, I become personalized behind my creations. When I write a book and go on television, they say, "Your name is Walter Starcke," and I say, "Yes, I am Walter Starcke." "You wrote this book?" I answer, "Yes, I wrote that book" and all the time, I am hiding behind my mask, becoming trapped in my mask.

Fortunately I have a bargain with life. I've been promised that before too long I will be put through what-ever is necessary to break up personal sense. In return, I have committed myself to taking time to feel the degree to which I am currently indulging in personal sense and promise to practice the disciplines necessary to break it up.

Life has become much simpler for me since I went through that tunnel and discovered my self-centeredness. I can now know at the end of any day just how much mask I have put on that day, how much personal sense I have allowed in order to be on the stage. Often I cannot take the mask off without stopping or resting for a while. I might have a moment of contemplation before going to bed but usually when I wake in the morning, I sit before my spiritual mirror and deal with my mask.

Life is simpler because I no longer spend much time trying to analyze the mask or even ask why I put it on. I simply see it in terms of crystallization. The mask of personal sense is like a crust. The object is to break up the crust, crack it, let it crumble. Like tartar on one's teeth, we become encrusted in a sense of self. Meditation is like daily flossing to slow down and break up the crust.

You would not be reading this if you had not already to some degree found the "double tread" between mask and true identity. Psychology may help you recognize and identify your mask. That's its main value. But mysticism, contemplation, meditation, surrender, and silence become the ways to drop the mask. Drop it just for a minute. However, if you spend too much time concentrating on the mask and studying it, the mask becomes too real and harder to eliminate.

Don't kid yourself. If you think people are people, if you go around giving personal advice, if you make human suggestions, if you localize or identify right and wrong, you are at the level of personal sense, at the psychological level. If so, like using an ice pick to chop up ice, you should apply the psychological laws of good conduct which apply to that situation and should not kid yourself into thinking you are being spiritual. You can't be spiritual about an effect, an appearance. Don't try. If you want to be spiritual, stop analyzing the human scene and just look at your spirit, the spirit of what you are doing and thinking, and switch dimensions. Because totalism, simultaneity, and transmutation exist; you can have it all and communicate with every level.

The Epistle to the Hebrews explains that if we are sons of God, we will be purged or scoured, "For what son is he whom the father chasteneth not?" In other words, our difficulties, our unpleasant experiences are God's flossing—breaking up personal sense—so that we can take our place as heirs to our Godliness. The unfortunate ones are those who are allowed to crystallize to such an extent that they are never naked of self, never spiritually mobile and free, but are trapped behind the crust of self, the mask.

Mantras and spiritual "one liners" are basically designed to break up personal sense. When I was in the Hindu monastery, I repeated the mantra, "Neti, neti," "Not this, not this, but thou, thou." It was my attempt to say, "Not this mask, not this mask, but the impersonal true spiritual being that I am."

So let our daily prayer be simple. Don't let our masks trick us into complicated mental gyrations. Simply become aware of the degree of our personal sense. Crack it up. Shake it off. Drop the mask. Communicate with your oneness of the spirit for the spirit doesn't mask anything nor can it be turned into a mask. Let all problems go because they are ALL masks. Spirit, spirit, spirit, is, is, is and when you have entered the silence of spirit, you are listening to yourself again without a mask. Enjoy that freedom for a while and then gird yourself about and dare to enter the world of personal sense once more, knowing that you can return to your source, take your mask off, and be at peace. That self-source is God.

The Metaphysical Leap

The realization of my own self-centeredness or the degree to which I was still involved with personal sense surprised me because I had long understood and talked about what I call the "metaphysical leap." The metaphysical leap is that moment when invisibles become more real and important to us than the visible forms we see with our eyes. After we have become aware that the cause is more important than the results, that the consciousness which creates is more important than what it creates, the invisible world of consciousness takes precedence over and becomes more of a reality than the visible world of effects. The world of spirit becomes more important and real than the world of effects.

Sometimes to make this point, I have said, "There aren't any people in the world. There are only states and stages of consciousness expressed in form." Of course, I see people, but the form they take isn't as important as who they are and what their consciousness represents.

After all, the scientists tell me that every cell in my body changes every seven years. I don't come along and say, "Walter number nine and a half says, 'Hello.' " I have had nine and a half bodies by now, as a material being. What's more, look at the pictures of me at various stages of my life and they represent totally different and almost indistinguishable forms. I've never been any of them. I have always been the consciousness within those forms. I have the forms but am not the form. I cut off my hair, cut my nails, shed my skin, and flush them down the toilet but I am still here because I am not, in fact, personal. People who really understand this principle are those who have made the metaphysical leap into invisible reality. Now, though they still inhabit the visible world, they are more aware of the reality of the invisible world of consciousness than the masks which appear in the world.

Everything that we see with our eyes belongs to the world of effects. It has been caused, or it wouldn't be here. It is not the cause itself. It is the result of a cause. It has been *personalized*. Mistakenly, we believe that appearances themselves are causes. We then lose sight of the real cause which is invisible.

This takes us back to the Gospel of St. John. "In the beginning was the Word, and the Word was with God, and the Word was God . . . And the Word was made flesh." But if we believe it stops being the Word because it has become flesh, we have missed the point.

Though it was personalized, it didn't stop being the Word. The idea which gives rise to a form remains "in" and "as" the form. The form itself isn't the most important part. What created it is. If you take away the idea, the form crumbles. The form only communicates the idea. Cause becomes visible as effect but the essence, the reality, and the truth of its being is still the consciousness which created it in the beginning.

Duality has communicated ignorance throughout history and we have falsely believed that the object and that which created it have become two separate things. We have believed that one is cause and the other is personalized flesh or effect. That belief loses sight of cause because it accepts effects as a separate reality and creates personal sense. Any time we are more aware of the effect than the cause, we are trapped in personal sense.

The "double thread" truth is this: that which is present, which has substance, is spiritual. Substance is spiritual when you see it free of personal sense but, when you believe it is material, you have personalized it and communicated a lie. You are seeing a distorted materialistic picture of what is here and have forgotten that it is really spirit formed. If you could see with what Jesus called "righteous judgment," you would not even see a so-called material world but rather a spiritual universe right here, right now. You'd see Heaven on earth and wouldn't be homesick anymore.

When Jesus talked about "this world," which is in opposition to "my kingdom," He was talking about the misinterpretation caused by personal sense, by material sense. In other words, the minute we personalize something or someone we cut our vision or communication off from the God's presence which is everywhere, all knowing, and all powerful.

When we reverse this personal sense and see with spiritual sense, the illusion of materiality evaporates, healings take place, harmony and peace reign. We are communicating with reality. As long as we strive and strain against "the slings and arrows of outrageous fortune," as Hamlet lamented, we are perpetuating personal sense. We only see reality when we take off the spectacles of personal sense. When we can look right at material things and see them as spirit formed, we are spiritually free.

It's like wearing a pair of cracked eye glasses. The world isn't actually cracked but when you observe the world through cracked lenses, everything seems to have a crack in it. When you personalize anyone or anything, you are distorting the picture just as though you were wearing cracked lenses. If your mind tricks you into trying to glue up the cracks, you are psychologically mesmerized. But if you take the glasses off, get rid of personal sense, you see perfection. You see that Heaven is here and you don't have to wait for it.

SEVEN

The Two Gods

With the stumbling block of our personal sense concept out of the way, we can communicate with an all-embracing God. Well, not really. We can't communicate with God if we still limit God solely to a personal sense concept. I feel that the single saddest misconception barring the way to Heaven for most people is the false or limited concept of God that most have been taught to accept. Unfortunately, many people who would really like to believe in God have altogether rejected God unknowingly because of their misconception.

I was called on the carpet once for using the word "God." It happened on one of my last trips to India. I made the tortuous journey from New Delhi up to the little town of Almora near the border of Tibet in that corner of India where India, Nepal, and Tibet come together. From there, I took the footpath to Lama Govinda's ashram. Lama Govinda and I had been friends since someone in England had sent him my book, *The*

Ultimate Revolution, claiming that it contained Tibetan wisdom. If so, it was probably because the book advocated the "double thread" approach which I now realize delightedly is also inherent in Tibetan teaching. At any rate, Govinda read my books, we began to correspond, and finally I visited him.

With a backdrop of the majestic Himalayas towering in the distance, this gentle, wise Lama and I were sitting on a bench beneath the pine trees sharing his clear no-nonsense wisdom when he stopped me. He said, "It would be better if you find a different word to use than the word 'God.' 'God' comes from the Hebrew concept which sees God as a father figure outside of yourself, other than yourself. It is impossible to use that word without thinking of a theistic God, something apart from you, not universal but personal. Find a new word." I thought for a second and suggested, "Lama Govinda. I know that many people mistakenly think of God as a punishing father figure sitting on a throne somewhere up in heaven but I don't think of God in that way myself. If I avoid the word, I would just be leaving it festering in the unconscious. If I want to eliminate the ignorance attached to the word, I must continue to use it in the way I conceive of it, hoping to clean up the old misconception."

The problem we have in our Hebrew/Christian background is that we've been taught *two* Gods, two different Gods—one true and one false—and we use them interchangeably. Unless we correct the misconception, we can't experience the truth.

I came to realize this clearly after I read a book *When Bad Things Happen to Good People* by Harold Kushner, a sensitive and dynamic Rabbi whose work has helped many people. Everything in the book made sense, too much sense because the more I read it, the worse I felt. I'm a good person. I may make some innocent mistakes, be self-centered at times, but I am as good as anyone I know. However, sometimes bad things happen to me. Why?

Based on the Old Testament book of Job, the Rabbi's explanation was all too logical. He meticulously pointed out the random nature of misfortune—how impossible it is to avoid the Russian roulette of good and bad. Concluding that God doesn't have control over everything, he settled for a limited and very depressing God. He claimed that God appears as those qualities in us which makes us noble in the face of desperation. God makes us able to take punishment. He claimed that God's way of appearing on earth is in terms of human resignation and our ability to take pain. Faith became more of an aspirin than a cause.

For a day or so, I carried the Rabbi's conclusions around with me and my feet were clothed in leaden shoes, tied to the earth. I know the Rabbi meant well and God does help us to be noble in the face of disaster but God is so much more.

Finally, I decided to look at the Rabbi's source for the answer, the book of Job itself. As usual, the answer wasn't so much in what the Scripture told me as what it didn't. Three verses leaped out at me which gave me the answer.

At the beginning, Job says, "For the thing which I greatly feared is come upon me, and that which I was afraid of is come unto me." In that statement, he placed himself under the law of fear or a graceless concept of God without even realizing it. His own fear set its own creations in motion. "That which I was afraid of is come unto me." He placed himself under the law of fear, the fearful God, and imaged it into being himself.

Another verse in Job says, "I looked for good, then evil came unto me: and when I waited for light, there came darkness." Now, we are getting closer to the key, the law of good and evil. When Adam and Eve ate of the tree of the knowledge of good and evil, our entire

Old Testament experience was born, born out of the belief in good and bad. Good and bad are logical. They make up the law. Our Adamic man of earth self can't understand anything else but the law. Grace is not logical, not mentally comprehendable. Fortunately, the law can lead one to grace in the end.

At the end of the story, God talks to Job, "Then will I also confess unto thee that thine own right hand can save thee." He didn't say that a God separate and apart from Job would save him but that which was within Job himself, "his own right hand" would. The God in Job could *save* him. In the end, Job came to know the true God and got rid of the false sense of God.

Through these three verses, I saw that Job had believed in a different God than the one Jesus taught. Job's God wasn't a God of grace. He was a God of law. He represented logic, the left brain. Everything had a logical cause-and-effect relationship. It related to "an eye for an eye and a tooth for a tooth" kind of reasoning. Job's God was a personal God.

Jesus's New Testament God of grace is one of spirit. There's spirit but no logic as such in the New Testament God. "If any man will . . . take away thy coat, let him have thy cloak also." That doesn't make sense. It isn't logical. You'd freeze to death.

I am not putting down logic or that rabbinical approach to God. It has its place because my "double thread" self has its Old Testament side and that side needs logic, needs a personal God. I consider myself to be both a Jew and a Gentile, as all of us who were born into the Hebrew/Christian culture are. My "man of earth" side is personal and needs to operate out of logic. If I can't get in touch with my Christ, my Spirit, then I have no choice but to live by logic and I had better reason psychologically. But if I limit myself just to a God of law, I will have the agonies Job had. I won't, if I can see how the two different concepts of God came about to begin with.

Creation

Perhaps the most important part of the whole Bible, because it defines God, is the creation story which is told in the first and second chapter of Genesis. There, both the true God and the false one emerge. Those first two chapters propose two totally different concepts of God.

The first chapter of Genesis announces a God of spirit who creates by imaging, not by logic. This God images light, images all the forms that inhabit the earth and they are good, not good as the opposite of bad but good as completion, wholeness, and *one*-ness.

This God-being "created man in his own image, in the image of God created he him; male and female created he them," both man *and* woman "in our own image" (plural, all one), equal and perfect, and gives them dominion—not subject to good and bad, not a toss of a coin existence, but dominion. God is spirit, formless, and creates spiritual being through the spirit of his imaging.

Now starting with the fourth verse of the second chapter of Genesis, the whole process of creation is told again but this time a different God does the creating, the "Lord God" outside of mankind. This God is never called just "God" or "spirit" or "us." This God is separate from mankind, exclusive of man. This God creates out of effects rather than spirit, out of materiality rather than the spirit. "The Lord God formed man of the dust of the ground." He created Adam out of dust. This Lord God made Adam stupid (asleep) and created a false concept of woman out of another effect, out of a bone, perhaps a bone of contention. Anyway, second-rate woman, subject to man, was this Old Testament God's creation.

Throughout the entire Old Testament, God is most often referred to as the "Lord God" of the second creation story. God and humankind are kept separate. They become antagonists (from the Greek, "antagonistes," meaning "in opposition").

I can see why Lama Govinda blenched at the use of a father-God. When people call God "Father," many of them are thinking of God as this Old Testament punishing Father, the Lord God, something apart from them, not the fathering spirit within.

If God were a supreme being separate from us, how could we either inherit His throne or be co-creators with Him? And He would certainly be too large to get inside of us where Jesus said the Father is.

As long as the prophets of the Old Testament labored under a false sense of God, they compounded the problem. They begged their followers to stop worshipping graven images. They wanted to clear up the superstition that God was in material effects, but as long as they still taught that God was the Lord outside of the individual, they themselves made an effect out of God. God is what created the creations and as long as we worship anything in the world of effect—thoughts, theologies, therapies, ikons, people, places, or any "thing"—we are worshipping the false God. When we see God as separate from us, we too have turned God into an effect.

It seems as though too much fuss is made over worshipping images but that's the *modus operandi* of freedom and communications. It is the key. We entertain images in our mind. Every thought is an image. Words are symbols, images. If we have a limited sense of God, that is what we image. We are always imaging. The point isn't that we should stop imaging but rather that we should appreciate the creative spirit of imaging without worshipping or honoring the God of effects.

We may think we are free from worshipping a false sense of God but as long as good and bad exist, we are imaging them and believing in two Gods. As long as we believe material things are neccessary, we are paying allegiance to the Old Testament God.

Surprising as it may seem, guilt is a form of worship. If I see myself engraved with personal sense, personal responsibility, personal shortcomings, I have imaged a self apart from God. God and I are no longer an "us." I honor that false graven image of myself every time I feel guilty. My guilt honors that image.

It's easy to see why a statement like the one in Hebrews could be seen in the Old Testament sense. It says, "It is a fearful thing to be in the hands of the living God." You can't hide behind the barn and cheat. Two and two are four and that's all there is to it. Mathametics doesn't punish you; you punish yourself. If you believe in a personal God who does punish, you have to live in fear because matters are not in your own hands just as they weren't in Job's until he found that his own right hand saved him.

Why God Won't

God is not in the human scene. The human scene is what Jesus was talking about when he said, "My kingdom is not of this world." "My kingdom" is the world of truth, love and purity. "This world" is what we see when we believe in a material interpretation of life, when we see both good and bad. It's the world of personal sense where bad things do happen to good people.

"My kingdom" (Heaven) is right here, right now. If we are not aware of it, that isn't because it isn't here. That's because we are looking at Heaven through the illusion of "this world." The human scene is the Old Testament interpretation of what is here; when we look at the world in "this world" terms, we are at a level which God doesn't know anything about. Truth doesn't know anything about lies because lies are not reality. They are nonexistent illusions about reality.

The real God doesn't know anything about illusion just as reality doesn't know anything about nightmares. When we are in the nightmare, the horrible things we see seem real to us but, when we wake up, they no longer exist.

God is like the sun. In terms of individual being, God is impersonal. God includes everything and everyone but doesn't think in terms of shining on this one and not on that one. The reason God doesn't know anything about good and bad is because we are all one wave-like being. There is no God separate from us. As the Psalm says, "If I ascend up into Heaven thou are there: if I make my bed in Hell, behold, thou art there."

When we believe in the false God, we can't release our problems. Release only happens by going beyond the war between good and bad, all of it. "This world" is a soap opera. The soap opera has an author called God, who plays with people's lives. But when we turn off the TV illusion of this false God, turn off our logical minds, we become the authors of our own lives. We are God's own selves, and nothing—no "thing"—can touch us to make a lie.

I can't tell you how many times I have been as near desperation as Job was, at the end of my rope. And in some unsuspected way, my mind has let go of looking for a God outside of myself or some other place than here, and before long I can't remember why I felt so bad, why I took it all so seriously. What's happened? Nothing. I just shifted channels from believing in the Old Testament God of good and bad and returned to

the God of grace in the first creation story. That's all.
I went from "this world" to "my kingdom" where God
and I communicate.

We talk a great deal about wanting to do the will
of God. As long as we think in terms of the will of
God, it shows that, to some degree, we still feel separate.
The will of God implies that there are two, my will
and God's will. So, as long as we are at the dual level,
we have to equally know both sides of the coin—what
God will and what God won't.

First and foremost, God won't "do" anything. To
some that may be a startling statement. We have all
been taught to think God is going to solve our problems,
to supply us, to protect us, to heal us, to fulfill us but
all these things are at the top of the list of what God
won't do anymore than mathematics will balance your
checkbook for you or the sun will shine because you
ask it to. They won't because the wave doesn't think
in terms of the particle. It just is. Mathematics just is.
The sun just is. It doesn't do anything. It just is. God
just is. God is a *be*-ing.

To believe that God will protect, heal, and supply
us shows several things: 1. that we believe God is our
servant; 2. that our interest is in getting rather than
in giving; 3. that we don't want to take responsibility
for our lives; and 4. that we don't know who we
are. If we did, we'd know that our own new mind is
God.

What God won't do is that God won't change,
won't give to one and not to another, won't be a servant,
won't take pity on us, won't be taken in by our ignorance
or our pleas. In other words, God won't appear in "this
world." God won't mess with the human scene. God
won't for a simple reason—*God can't*. If we really understood the impersonal nature of God, we'd stop trying
to bring God down to the personal level where it can't
be. We'd stop trying to make truth enter the lie.

"God is too pure to behold iniquity." So how can it operate at that level? God can't become because God already is perfection. Anything that is being can't become, it already is. Truth can't do anything. It just is. Truth won't do anything for me. If there is any doing, I must do it, because truth or God won't and can't.

If I lock myself into a closet, the sun can't come in and heal me. If I add incorrectly and give away all my marbles, mathematics can't help me. Mathematics, truth, and God are impersonal. They don't operate at the level of my problems. Problems only appear at a personal level. I am personal so if there is any solving, it's up to me, God won't.

Ah, but that doesn't leave me without all the healing magic of God or the useful truth inherent in mathematics. If I transcend *this world* of ignorance and enter the kingdom of truth I have access to all the heavenly riches.

Because of this truth, straight and narrow is the path and few there be that enter. Few people want to take the responsibility, few accept that God won't. You have to *DO* God's will because "God won't" means that you yourself have to become all you thought God was. That's too overwhelming for most of us. But the "awe-full" truth is that if we want healing, peace, protection, and all the other goodies of life, we have to do the doing by entertaining God in our consciousness because God won't unless we do. If we, in our particle sense, want to have all that is included in God, we have to bond with God. And we begin bonding by realizing what God won't or can't do. God can only be.

Of course, without God being, without the truth, we can't do anything, either. But the truth can't do without us as well. That's what co-creatorship and co-communication with God mean. We must entertain the truth in our consciousness. We must be the truth in action. Then, when the truth is alive in our consciousness, the crooked places will indeed be made straight, the eyes of the blind will open, the kingdom of Heaven will appear on earth and we won't be homesick any more—all because God won't.

Because God won't, we have a reason to grow and become. We would never consciously realize that God is our individual being and that we are how God appears on earth if we were not required to be the truth in action.

Rejoice, we are not helpless. God won't because God can't *unless* we allow God into our consciousness. We are the windows that allow the light into the world. Without our individual windows, God—the light—cannot enter the world. We have the new mind, the mind of God, within us. It is indeed impersonal and abstract but the miracle is that we can contact that withinness and it will manifest itself at the personal level. That's the paradox. We can't go to it personally but if we "know aright" we can tap into the source. When we do, we realize that it isn't "I go before you to make the crooked places straight" as though God will, but rather, "I go before you to reveal there are no crooked places."

I'll admit that what I have been doing is tearing down a limited personal-sense God in order to make the infinite ever-present God available. So now that we have accepted that God won't, let's find out what God will.

EIGHT

The Will of God

Now I have a problem. This is where I have to start lying. I know that "if you can name God, it isn't." Nevertheless, here I go trying to put into words what can only be experienced. First of all, I must see and experience God in all the ways I also experience my own total and multi-dimensional being. If I am multi-dimensional, then God certainly is as well. That means God appears at each dimension in terms of that dimension, in the form that dimension can comprehend and appreciate. God has as many faces as there are levels of comprehension. Every concept of God has something to say for itself and has validity at some level. What we have to do is keep from limiting ourselves to any one understanding of God.

When I am at my lowest or most personal level, you can bet your life I reach out to a personal God, as a father figure if you wish. When I am locked in personal sense and someone offers me an abstract principle, I feel desperate and deserted. I want a Father, a God into whose lap I can crawl with His arms around me. That's the God most of us were brought up to believe in, a theistic God. If we destroyed that concept of God in order to experience all the other dimensions of God, we would be cheating ourselves because there will always be a time when we need a personal relationship with God, but neither should we cut ourselves off from the mystical union with God. Most of us don't need to contemplate a personal God as much as to become more aware of the God within so that the internal God becomes as much a reality as the external one.

When Jesus said that He was in God and God was in Him and that our relationship was a kind of partnership with God, a co-creatorship, He was trying to decondition the Old Testament concept of God and make God less a matter of chance or "here today, gone tomorrow."

When I finally came to experience God as a more procedural God, the process of a divine order, I was no longer inhibited by a punishing, withholding, or judgmental God whose blessings depended on my finding the right words to say or the right candle to light. That is why I am going to spend more time explaining God as the divine plan which has been such a help to me.

My first opening to an awareness of a less personal but more infinite sense of God came when I was taught the three words most metaphysical teachings apply to God, the three O words—omniscient, omnipresent, omnipotent. It makes sense that to be infinite, God would have to be all knowing, everywhere, and all powerful.

I've just now discovered, however, how linear even those words are. If I say "God is omniscient," that statement could mean that there is a super being sitting in that great library in the sky with his finger on all knowledge. Then if I believe God is omnipresent, I could be believing that God is materially present as an effect and therefore localized in time and space. If I say God is omnipotent, the only power, I picture God as a power which is over some other power, so it isn't in fact the only power. An omnipresent, omniscient, omnipotent God can still be seen as Job's God.

But (and I know I am indugling in naughty dialectics) if I say that "God is omni-science, omni-presence, and omni-potence," that is another matter. I can think of God as an "everywhereness" without particalizing God because, the wave is everywhere and not localized. I can think of God as omniscience because it doesn't take much of a leap of imagination to conceive of the fact that an accumulation of infinite intelligence does exist. Whether I am able to tune into it or not is another matter. Then if I think of God as omnipotence, just as raw creativity itself, not being over anything but just all-potent movement, all life, all beingness, I realize God is something which I can experience. God is experiential, not mental or cluster, not linear.

If I can realize God as everywhereness, I can be aware that "The ground on which I stand is holy ground" and I am hopeful with possibility.

If I can realize God is all knowledge and I, being a particle, am connected to that all-knowing wave, I can inevitably tune in to it and "be" that knowledge myself, have access to that knowledge myself.

But omnipotence is another matter; that's where I stumbled. How could I believe God is omnipotent when I saw so much evil? Yet it is the one of the three *O* words that is by far the most important to know.

I can remember the exact moment when I got a feel for God's being the one and the only power. Sure the concept began to form in my mind when I sat before the Needle on Maui way back at that initial breakthrough but it wasn't until some years later before the "click" took place which made the concept other than something that insulted my intelligence.

At that point, I had a New York apartment in the Des Artists off Central Park by the Tavern on the Green, a proper setting for a successful young producer. There I was in my grandeur, a twenty-two foot ceiling in my sky-lighted living room, an antique Samurai sword and a collection of fine paintings on the walls, my car parked in the garage—and I was miserable. It was one of those times when meditation didn't help. I tried everything and, when nothing else worked, I reverted to my early Methodist background and got down on my knees and begged to a personal God. Low and behold, I was answered with an impersonal principle which has done more than anything else to help me to know how I could love God.

When I looked up from my kneeling position, my eyes focused on a light bulb. My inner voice began one of its lectures. It said, "See the light bulb? What makes the light? It is the action and reaction of the plus and minus currents hitting against each other that causes the light. To human sense, the light seems to result from the interaction of two powers, two forces, contesting each other, but in fact what you are seeing is not duality at all, it is *polarity*." It went on to explain, "In the visible world of personal sense, there are always two, good and bad, plus and minus currents. That is all personal sense can comprehend, but in the invisible, in the abstract, there is only one principle of electricity. There is only *one power*, one electricity. What looks like destructive negativity at one moment is part of creativity. Actually it is only the movement of transmutation, of polarity, oneness not duality."

I realized then that there had been many, many times in my life when I had thought that bad had won out over good, that accidents happened, that mistakes had been made. Looking back, I could see a creative pattern. Everything had been neccessary for my growth and ultimate good. Of course, as a human, I could not always see that ultimate progress because I was still locked into time and space. Humanly, I also thought that death was a reality, but in cosmic terms, there is only one steady blossoming of the divine plan.

When I saw the principle, I knew how to love God. It was so simple. I didn't need to whip up some false emotion called love. There was something I could do which was an act of love. Every time I believe there is a power apart from omnipotence, a power apart from God, I can realize I am not loving God and stop it. Every time I look right at disturbing appearances, every time I read disturbing headlines and smile knowing that what I am seeing is polarity, not duality—and refused to fear—I am loving God. The recognition that there is no power but God is how I love God.

Until this day, whenever I fear, whenever I doubt, whenever I believe evil can triumph over good, whenever I become aware of disturbing circumstances, I know I must not judge the appearances at face value or I am not loving God. Sometime I may sound like Pollyanna trying to rationalize discord, sometime it may take me a while to get back in love with God, but now I know how. God is the only power and, despite appearances, sooner or later the divine plan will be revealed.

The Divine Process

Anyway, in this day of labels, believing God is "theistic" makes God too transcendant, too overwhelming, and places God outside of us. The "pantheistic" label limits God too much to the world of effects and localizes God; so I put the two together to create a "double thread" word, "panentheistic," both imminent and transcendant, particle and wave. Maybe it's another of my "how to have your cake and eat it" words, but I like it.

It's easy to convert so-called atheists to this all-inclusive sense of God. All you have to do is ask if they accept the fact that there is some process behind life. Both the atheists and the agnostics will admit that there is an order in the universe. Unless they are playing dialectic games, they admit that as far as they are aware, the sun rises in the morning at a specific time, winter follows fall, not summer, an ordinary human gestation takes nine months, and so on. In other words, there is an order.

Every creative act, from planting a garden to baking a cake, has an order, a priority of steps, a sequence, a season. If the souffle is put in the oven before it is properly mixed, it won't rise. When we get out of order, we fall flat. The execution of this order, this divine order, if you will, is called the "process." We can forget all the fancy words for God because God is simply the divine *process* and anyone who recognizes this process in life is necessary for growth is admitting that God exists.

Mankind has come a long way in dissecting and understanding process. We have broken the atom and analyzed its order, we have discovered the DNA order in the genetic code, but we have only scratched the surface of an understanding of divine order. So we arrive at a fundamental decision. Do we limit our trust just to the degree of order that we can understand with our minds? Does our survival depend on our figuring out the proper sequences in life? Or do we trust that there is a divine order and that when we trust it and are in step with it, we will rise, even from the grave as Jesus did?

"Thy will be done" translates into "I want to follow the divine order." Perhaps that is what it means when the scripture says, "Strait is the gate and narrow is the way which leadeth unto life, and few there be that find it." The sequence is so precise that only those who have surrendered their personal sense to it and those who are open to *hear* can follow it to perfection.

I can't consciously understand the divine sequence but
I can be aware of it, feel it, and experience its order.

There's nothing I can do to change, alter, or affect
divine order. I can't speed it up nor slow it down. But
when I feel fear, depression, futility, or lack, there is
something I can do. I can dispel the illusion that there
is a power other than divine order and trust the process.
All I can do is to release the sense of separation I have
from the divine process, God.

At any given moment, something is beating my
heart, moving my fingers, digesting my food. All of
those functions are happening as part of the physical
process that is going on "in" and "as" myself. It doesn't
stop just with my physical self, however. The process
is bringing into my presence whatever I need. It is directing to me the next person who will enter the door of
my consciousness. The process is showing me the next
step I must take. The process is leading me to the next
profession I am to practice. The process is preparing
the next lesson I am to learn.

Everything, absolutely everything, is alive, as Theil-
hard de Chardin so beautifully put it. The process is
working throughout all the universe. It isn't a matter
of whether it will provide or not. It's a matter of whether
I trust it or not.

Any pressure or fear I have reflects how I relate
to the divine process. When I pray for help or guidance,
I may believe, "I am reaching out to God." That may
not comfort me, but if I realize I am trying to contact
the "process," I can feel something. We can experience
the process. We can trust the process as an act of will.
When we do, we are loving God.

When scared, fearful people reach out to someone
or some church and are told to "trust God," often a
helpless bewilderment overwhelms them. Trusting God
seems to be a blind abandonment of a personal effort,
an abdication of responsibility to some superstitious

power off in space somewhere. At those times, it insults the mind. So many people have prayed millions of prayers to this God with few results. Trusting a superstitious concept of God is a kind of spiritual poker game. "Maybe" replaces self-determination.

If, however, some people come to you needing help and you can get them to see God expressing Himself in their bodies, minds, and experiences as an automatic, ever-present, consistent, impersonal, available, maintaining, sustaining process working equally for everyone, saint or sinner, irrespective of place, understanding, or capacity, then there is something they can do. They can trust the process. Observing God as process removes superstition.

The word, "process" comes from the Latin, "pro" meaning "forward" and "cedere" meaning "to go," to go forward, to proceed. To have faith in God means to have faith in being able to go forward, to proceed.

The wonderful thing about trusting the process is that though the process is impersonal, you can feel it personally. When the chips are down, you either trust God or you don't because God *is* the process of life. You don't have to speculate whether you really have faith or not. If you trust the process, you have faith.

The Biblical Code

Understanding God as process has helped me crack the Biblical code as well. The Bible is full of references to God as the divine process. To begin with, the Bible says that the Father is within. Something is beating my heart, hearing through my ears, growing me, processing me. Yes, the process is certainly working within me. I need not "take thought for the morrow," matters outside of myself. My life is the process.

The Bible says, "I will go before thee, and make the crooked places straight." That "I" is the process.

Like mathematics, the process has a starting point, a proceeding, and a result. A peach tree has a blossom and the fruit process goes before it to evolve a tiny green ball, grow it into a soft ripe fruit, and drop it into our lap, all the process. If I do not trust that process, I would never plant a peach tree.

"Your father knoweth what thing ye have need of" and "It is your father's good pleasure to give you the kingdom." The process knows what the next step is and it is the pleasure of the process to take care of each step.

"Speak, Lord; for thy servant heareth" means "Process reveals my next step to me because it is my wish to follow the process." This is a co-creatorship between me and the process, so let me do my part, give me my instruction.

The process says, "Take therefore no thought for the morrow." You can only do what is next and when the following step comes, the process will show you what to do then. Trust the process and it will cloth, feed, and house you not because of superstition but because of an automatic cause and effect relationship.

When self-doubt enters, remember you too *are* the process. Perhaps you are not yet a perfect fruit, a perfect result of the process, even your shortcomings are being eliminated, worked out, brought forward, as a part of the process.

Look back; you are not the same as you were years ago. The process has brought you forward all along and will complete it "unto the day of Jesus Christ," meaning until you are that perfect example of what the process creates.

"Be still and know that I am God." Be still and know that the reconciling process is proceeding within. Process is movement, process is healing, process is love. Process reconciles the visible and the invisible. When we hear to love God and have a hard time identifying, we can picture a divine process trying to help us at every minute and love that fact. Trusting the process is loving God.

I remember a time years ago when I thought I was at my rope's end. I was far from any feeling of spiritual presence and was so depressed I could hardly move. Someone said, "Just keep functioning." Though I couldn't accept spiritual truth at that time, that statement was a mental crutch I could lean on. I blindly hung on to it with the hope that if I kept functioning, something would happen. Because there was actually a spiritual principle involved, because there is a divine process, it worked and little by little the flow of life began and increased until I was alive again. God was alive in my life.

Yes, there is a narrow line. First, we must sense the process, tune in to it, feel it. Then we must flow with it but not try to force it. Holding back and not moving with it, not moving with God, is wrong. But pushing ahead, trying to force our will—fearing that the process won't be on time—is almost worse than doing nothing.

Again, there are the two commandments. To love God is to trust the process and to love neighbor is to physically aid the process in material ways. It's both. The Trinity is made up of the process, me, and the spirit that flows when we are in tune with each other.

Let me get personal again. I woke up one morning confused about what to do next and was tempted to look beyond the day into a dubious future. When I sat down to pray, the Lord's prayer come out like this:

Our Creator, divine order, which art the perfect process of being, holy be thy recognition, thy sequence be done, at the material level as it is in spirit. Give us each day the process which nourishes the order, forgive us when we try to change the divine process, as we forgive others who try. Lead us not into the temptation to doubt the divine process, deliver us from the hypnotism of doubt, for the divine order is the kingdom, the power, and the glory of all being.

Surrender Closes the Gap

Dying daily means surrendering to the process daily, surrendering personal responsibility. As long as we keep thinking of ways to solve our problems, of steps which we can take so that something will happen, we have not yet completely surrendered. Even our attempts to find a spiritual answer show we have not surrendered to trust in the process.

Paradoxically, surrendering to the process seems like an immobile, defeated, and inactive performance, but it is just the opposite. Remember, the word "process" means "to go forward." When we surrender to the process, we do not stay in one spot. We are not inactive, we go forward.

As I have said so often, "A Christian proceeds not only despite appearances but regardless of consequences." That means that the ultimate trust is in trusting our actions despite what our minds see and conjecture.

There is never a time when we can't put one foot in front of another. This is the principle behind the Biblical story of the widow who had only a pot of oil. Elisha told her to begin to "pour," which meant "trust the process, proceed." As she poured her little pot of oil, the infinite flow was opened. She did it by co-creating with the process.

The "double thread" approach means to work with what is at hand, all of it. We have our minds and corresponding mental energy. We have our bodies manifesting physical energy, and we have our latent spiritual energy which is the divine process. As I said before, we can't hurry or delay it but we can take whatever is at hand and work with that. We can use them all singly and collectively. When one dimension seems weak, we can reinforce it with the others. We never reject any, but when all seem low, then final trust comes in, God comes in. We allow the process to take over.

Simpleminded God

The trouble with trying to explain an all-being God is that we increasingly complicate its all inclusive simplicity. I remember one time when I was at a conference and was asked to talk to a group of four to six year olds. I didn't know what to say so I started out asking, "What's God?" One little boy screwed up his face, looked at me as though I was stupid, and said, "God is everything." That put me in my place.

The wisest know that God is the simple mind. Simple means single, one. It comes from the Latin word "simplex" which means oneness. To be single-minded is to be simple-minded. If God is omniscience, all know-ingness, there isn't more than one, and one is the ultimate simplicity. Obviously then simplicity is the key to Godliness.

The wisest person is the one who is able to convey the most with the fewest words. The greatest artist is the one who can express the greatest truth with the fewest strokes of the brush. Simplicity reveals the master.

What's the opposite of simplicity? Complication. Complication comes from the Latin word, "complecti" meaning "to encircle" and its synonyms are "abstruse, confused, entangled, intricate, and involved." That says it all. Personal sense is the opposite of God because personal sense is always complicated. Explanations are complicated.

Way back when I was new to the metaphysical adventure and ready to launch into lengthy dissertations at the drop of a hat, I used to visit a favorite uncle of mine in Texas. He was a loving soul who lived a simple and therefore pure life on a farm beside a river. He was a reformed alcholic who spent forty years helping others. He would let me spin my wheels for a while, then he would gently tell me, "Keep it simple, keep it simple." Oh, how right! And I still haven't managed as I would like.

The simplemindedness of God isn't accidental. Complexity is grown from the accumulation of things. Thoughts are things. Whenever we are caught up in things, we are caught up in complexity and simplicity is forgotten. We get caught in a web of words.

It's the old eye of the needle again. You can't get a bunch of threads through the eye of a needle and you can't get a bunch of thoughts or problems through it either. God is one, "1," like a single thread, one stroke. The letter "I" is essentially the same sign as the numeral "1," one stroke. Simplicities can go through the eye. Even though one thread may be made up of several strands, when they are united as one, there is simply one thread.

How does this apply to my daily dilemma? My problem is deep or complex in direct proportion to the number of things, thoughts, or concerns involved. Complexity is a sure sign that my focus is on *this world* at the level of personal sense. Now is the time to drop it, to drop all the its and get back to the simplicity of God.

We may be able to narrow our problem down to a simple answer but the chances are that the problem only exists because of complications to begin with. So once more we turn to the simplicity of God, oneness, the divine process. We keep our focus on oneness. We remember that the Lord God is a jealous God. That means it won't stand the competition of other thoughts and ideas apart from the divine one.

God is simple because there are no things involved. God is simple because it is all inclusive as one and therefore only oneness has to be experienced. The minute I think it is up to me to make the decision, I am in complexity.

Have you ever seen what you might call highly evolved or saintly persons who didn't appear open and simple? At least, you feel their attention is one-pointed, their minds reflect the serenity of simplicity, peace prevails.

Trust and simplicity go hand in hand. When a complex problem appears, the temptation is to believe we must solve it but every thought multiplies geometrically. If trust is there, we can realize that the simplicity of God will resolve the complexity, and concentrate on letting go rather than adding to.

God Knows, God Knows

When someone asks us a question for which we have no answer, we say, "God knows." "God knows, God knows" is a way of reminding ourselves that our finite mind cannot comprehend omniscience.

I'm always tempted to seek something from God. But I know that God just is and that there is only one thing I can legitimately seek from God and that is God itself. God is divine cause, cause itself. It's natural and easy to think of results, effects, and to seek them rather than God, who is actually their cause. Say, for instance, that we need to pay our bills and have no money. Naturally we start to pray for money but money is an effect and if we pray for it, we pray amiss.

We can get to the point where we observe a need in terms of effects. That can signal us to stop thinking at the level of effects and open ourselves for the experience of cause. God is not money, God is "supply" itself. God is not a servant, God is fulfillment itself. Supply, fulfillment, and completion are essences, qualities, not effects.

Yes, it is possible to enter the silence and to experience supply without thinking of money, to experience fulfillment without thinking of a problem or lack. God is direction, God is harmony, God is fulfillment, and God is all knowing.

I don't have to tell God my problem. My problem is an effect. I don't have to tell God my need. Infinity cannot be minus anything. That means God includes everything in its knowingness. God knows.

When I remember God knows, it reminds me that I don't need to take my problem to God, I don't need to tell God anything. I do need to claim, not to tell but to claim. What do I need to claim? God. I need to claim fulfillment, wholeness, health, harmony, supply, and direction. All of those are qualities of God. Have God, and I have Heaven.

I know, it's really hard for personal sense to accept but we never get anything *from* God. Everything is included *in* God. God *is* what we want. God *is* the peace, God *is* the joy, God *is* the harmony, God *is* the supply, God *is* the love. If God is in us, we have all those things in us, but praying for them creates exactly the opposite because it implies that they are not already included in us.

God's Thoughts

God is the only creator (God is the process of creation), therefore God is the only thinker. If you are thinking, it is the God in you that is thinking. All ideas come from God, but distortion takes place when ideas are interpreted through personal sense.

Like the growth of a plant, the seed of an idea is planted in consciousness and then it evolves from the invisible to the visible. Every seed has a divine and creative purpose. When all the conditions are right, it will grow into fruition and produce a loving effect. By that I mean that every thought as it is created is potentially designed to heal, to manifest harmony, cooperation, and union. But when an idea appears as a personal creation rather than from God, it takes on the color of personal judgment, personal desire. When that happens, the creative energy latent in the thought is directed into separation, division, and possibly destruction. It is no longer God's divine idea but nevertheless its power is borrowed from the truth of its source.

That's why I keep saying, "The mind shouldn't be a thinking instrument but rather a seeing instrument." The mind should be used as an avenue of awareness, a tool to implement creativity, and not as a judging personal possession. The mind should be the telephone we use to communicate with God.

When I stop believing that my own personal sense is the creator, when I allow God's thoughts to become my thoughts, then I do God's will. How do I do that?

First, when a thought appears in my consciousness, I must know the truth about the thought ("Ye shall know the truth, and the truth shall make you free"). I ask, "Does this thought come from God, my new mind?" If the answer is "yes," then I can be impersonal about it and possibly see what it is saying to me.

Second, even if I begin the thought with personal sense and it seems fearful or destructive, I can remember that God's thoughts always have a loving purpose. I look through the thought to see how it can be helpful. I don't just denounce the thought. I uncover its meaning.

For example, if I have a negative thought about my partner, I can realize that it's negative and not a

God thought. I must have personalized myself and/or my partner. The thought started with God but personalization distorted it. If I can stand aside and look at the thought impersonally, I may see it as a cry for love. Behind that seed-thought or cry is a truth that can free both myself and my partner.

The only obstacle I need to overcome is the personal reaction—not the seed-thought. If I can get my personal sense interpretation out of the way, God's perfect idea can be manifested through me or *as* me.

As a matter of fact, that perfect idea needs me as much as I need it. An idea needs my mind, my body and my intellect in order to express itself. When I realize that every thought comes from my God self and I let God interpret and fulfill that thought through me, harmony and love result.

Attitudes are symbolized in the word that we comprehend. If I have the attitude of love, I am able to see the word as that which God created—and the resultant effect reflects my attitude in loving harmony.

Self-love cannot be dependent on what another thinks of you. If you love yourself because of what another thinks of you, you are not the thinker and God is not the thinker. All thoughts are love in transition, in evolution. All thoughts are fragments of truth returning to the one. If we see them as complete within themselves, we divide the one. If we see thought as God manifesting the one, we create the one. So it is very important that we see all thoughts as God's thoughts.

Man is co-creator because the invisible God needs to become visible and that happens through us as the bridges. Consciousness is invisible idea, the word, and the word becomes visible through thought. We are the tools through which creation is chiseled. It is chiseled through thought. Therefore we must realize the power inherent in thought, but be aware of channeling God's meaning and quality, thereby producing Godly results.

We do that in direct proportion to the extent to which we can impersonalize. Personal sense is the lens through which thoughts appear. If we are impersonal, there is nothing blocking the pure God form. Jesus was so impersonal that we see him as the Word itself. There was no personal sense in him to block the pure Word. That's why his words were God's words.

To claim our inheritance is to see all our thoughts as God's thoughts. To claim our inheritance is to realize that behind all our thoughts are truth, power, and fulfillment.

Wow

My Thoughts

Now I am going to turn right around and contradict myself, or seem to. That's the problem with the simultaneous awareness necessary for the "double thread."

Before I went into my dark night experience, I used to listen, hoping for God's thoughts to be revealed to me. I felt God spoke to me as though I was "here" and God was "there." When my guidance cut out, I thought it would never reappear and it didn't in the way it had been conceived before.

When I began to get inner guidance once more, it was different from what it had been before when I was still caught up in self-centeredness. Before it had been God *and* me, as though God was other than included in my being. Now it was all incorporated in my wholeness. I was no longer hearing something apart from myself as though it was speaking to me. It was as though God was no longer outside of me, but was now within. Now my thoughts were God's thoughts. I listen to myself, my real self, *my new mind*. My new mind, your new mind, the new mind are all the same. I was listening to the process. It is abstract, impersonal, and universal. So when I am listening to my third eye mind, whatever operates the pineal, I am listening to God's thoughts because they are in me and are my own thoughts.

Sure, I still have conversations with myself but now it is me, my neighbor self, talking to me, my God self.

Stand up, claim wholeness, fulfillment, harmony, and the truth that there is no idea other than God's, and that is your own new mind. Acknowledge God as the presence, law, cause, and activity of all that is, and stop trying to manipulate it physically or mentally in the without. Get back inside yourself, and there resolve all appearances. That's not saying you should ignore appearances or turn your back on them. I'm saying to reconcile them with the wave.

The law of illusion is what we call "the first law of human nature," the law of survival. You might call it the law of loneliness. The law of survival says, "This is good; it will perpetuate my personal sense. That is bad; it will separate me from others."

The law of truth or God is much more difficult. It's what I call the "first law of spiritual nature." Few preach it and fewer still want to practice it because it won't let you hide. You can't blame your wife. You can't blame your government. You can't blame the communists. You can't blame the stock market. You can't even blame God. The first law of spiritual nature is:

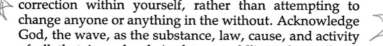

There is never a conflict with person or condition, but rather a false concept mentally entertained about person, thing, circumstance, or condition. Therefore, make the correction within yourself, rather than attempting to change anyone or anything in the without. Acknowledge God, the wave, as the substance, law, cause, and activity of all that is and refrain from meddling physically or mentally in the without. Go back inside of yourself, in your God mind, and there resolve all appearances.

Few people have the strength to accept this law because it doesn't let them off the hook. There's no one to blame, and few churches dare to preach it because ultimately it will put them out of business if it is heard.

Sure, I still go to the office and I bellyache if I have a problem like anyone else. I'll grumble about injustice, even blame others, and some people will say, "Look, he doesn't live the things he talks about," but I promise you that, when I go home and enter my closet, so to speak, I don't blame anyone for anything. I recognize that whatever happens to me stems from my own consciousness or it couldn't be in my life.

Everything in my life is the out-picturing of my own consciousness. If I want to change the outer picture, I have to change what caused it, my own consciousness. When I see disturbances, I don't try to change the picture I change my mind.

"A thousand shall fall at thy side and ten thousand at thy right hand," said the Psalmist, but destruction will not come nigh the one who lives "in the secret place of the Most High." What's the secret place? It's the new mind. Knowing this intellectually doesn't help unless we know how to experience the new mind and that is where prayer comes in.

PART II

The Experience

NINE

The Paradox of Prayer

When I first started seriously studying the Bible, I avoided the Old Testament. It was too confusing. I loved soaking up the mysticism of the New Testament, but the Old Testament upset me. When I got to "I Am" in the Gospel of St. John, I was in Heaven. That's where I wanted to live. As time went on, I realized that the two Testaments were really connected. They together constituted a "double thread."

The Old Testament is like the pieces of an automobile, all separated and scattered around the yard. Every aspect of human nature is expressed and detailed. It is as confusing and alarming as life itself. The Old Testament leads you up all kinds of alleys, contradicts itself, and is inconsistent, to say the least. All the pieces of the machinery to transport us through life are there, but no one knows how to put them together so that the machine works. Then along comes Jesus, the "master" mechanic, who takes all the elements, all the Scriptures of the Old Testament and joins them or interprets them in an order that will come to life. He doesn't invent as much as He assembles. As I said earlier, he reveals that the Old represented the psychological and all its laws, the New the mystical and its healing magic. He gives us the priority, grace, and with it eternal life. Of course, there are some overlaps. Jesus started with psychological instruction because He had to prepare His followers for mysticism. Then He lifted them into an experience of the Christ.

In a similar, though hardly comparable way, I see now that this book, *Homesick for Heaven*, is divided into those two divisions. Up until now, I have presented the pieces of the puzzle of human and divine identities and the need to communicate. It has been like packing a bag in preparation for a journey. Now I would like to show how to start the motor and how the journey has proceeded in my own life.

If there is one urgent message which Jesus tried to offer, it is the neccessity of prayer, the power of prayer, and the proper way to pray in both thought and action. Prayer is like turning the key. Without prayer, the motor won't run.

I really hurt when I see people trying desperately to pray, knowing that they have been taught a false sense of prayer and most likely their prayers will result in exactly the opposite of what they want. Sometimes their way of praying does more to create the thing they fear than to eliminate it.

Ever since religion was invented, people have been praying superstitiously with remarkably poor results. Considering the number of prayers that are offered each day in countless churches and prayer groups with so few visible successes, it's surprising they continue. Nevertheless, people continue to meet in public places to pray either out of fear or as though they are hopefully paying the premium on a kind of divine insurance policy. If they took prayer as seriously as they take their business problems, by this time they would have realized how spiritually bankrupt they were and would look for a new method for getting harmonious results.

The Phonies

Before anyone can pray "aright," they have to stop praying "awrong." When Jesus said our prayers would be answered, he always said they would if we pray in the right way.

I'll tell you how to spot phony prayer, the kind the Pharisees and hypocrites pray. Examine which God they are worshipping, the God of Job which is outside themselves or the God of the New Testament which is within.

When people pray, "Dear God, help Mary Jane who has breast cancer," right away you can see that they are not only malpracticing Mary Jane by losing sight of her true identity but their words show that they conceive of God as a being off in the clouds who lacks omniscience and is so ill-informed that He has to be told what Mary Jane's problem is. He also has to be told exactly who needs help, and is so *non compos mentis* that he has to be told to do His job. Right away that contradicts the all-knowing God who includes every bird in the air or every leaf on the trees.

When, as some prayer groups do, people believe that God needs to be informed of the address where help is needed, this too implies God doesn't even know where to go without a road map and therefore isn't omnipresent. When people think they have to tell God what illness a person has, it implies God won't or can't heal that person without knowing what kind of medicine is needed. That not only insults God's intelligence but implies that God is indeed not omnipotence nor omniscience, but rather is a kind of fighting machine who must rush over and take on some other evil power at some place where He is not currently present.

Perhaps the word "prayer" is the wrong word to use anyway. "To pray" comes originally from the Latin word, "precari" meaning "to beg." Instead of spelling it "pray," they should spell it "prey" for that is what it is for most people, an attempt to prey on God, or get *from* God, what they want.

I have a hard time sitting in many church services, because to me the way they pray is a sacrilege. The word "sacrilege" comes from the Latin "sacrilegium" meaning "to rob or take away the sacred." The "preyers" who tell you to look outside of yourself for God, take away your sacred right to find it within yourself.

When Jesus said, "Ye shall neither in this mountain nor yet at Jerusalem, worship the father," or "When thou prayest, enter into thy closet," he was saying to enter your own new mind for that is the only true place to pray. Anyone who tells you to pray to something outside of yourself is a phony. Any minister or prayer group which encourages you to pray "for" any thing, any leader who tells you to make your prayers into a personal sense plea is committing a sacrilege against you. They are robbing you of God. Look at the spirit of that kind of petitionary prayer. It's paranoid. It's based on fear. It wants. Ultimately, it wants your soul.

Promises, promises, promises. Petitionary prayers are attempts to blackmail God. "God, give me what I want and I will have faith in you." The only true prayer is the recognition that God already *is*. It is that recognition which changes appearances for, if God is omnipresence, omnipotence, and omniscience, there can be nothing else but God. Prayer should be the acknowledgment of "my kingdom."

The Lord's Prayer

Now I am really going to step on some sacred toes! I'm going to expose the wrong way of saying the Lord's Prayer. From the time I was a small boy, I repeated the Lord's Prayer daily, though superstitiously, I expect. I knew Jesus told us that this is how we should pray, but in my youth I wasn't aware that there were two different concepts of God and how that affected the attitude of my prayer.

Presently I realize that the kingdom of God is either right here, right now, or it never was and never will be. So when I "listen" to the Lord's Prayer, I hear it in a different way than I use to. I hear it as recognition, not as wishful thinking. What changed was my realization that prayer has to be an acceptance of Heaven as being right here, right now, not an attempt to make it so in the future.

Prayers that put Heaven off in the future are Job's prayers. We all have a Job self and the commonly accepted interpretation of the Lord's Prayer relates to that self. Remember, the "Lord" God is the God of the second creation story. Jesus didn't call it the Lord's Prayer. His translators did. And I suspect He didn't voice it as though there was a God outside of Himself or a Heaven that was not now.

Let me show you how Job would have interpreted the Lord's Prayer, "Our Father which art in heaven" (but not on earth), "Hallowed be thy name" (as though it isn't already Holy), "Thy Kingdom come" (as though it hasn't yet), "Thy will be done" (as though there is any other will than God's), "On earth as it is in heaven" (two different worlds), "Give us this day our daily bread" (as though God would withhold it or needed to be asked), "Forgive us our debts" (as though they were not already forgiven), "As we forgive our debtors" (or those who trespass against us—when actually no one can trespass against us), "And lead us not into temptation" (as though God would deliberately guide us into temptation), "but deliver us from evil" (making evil a reality). Finally it acknowledges, "Thine is the kingdom, and the power, and the glory for ever."

There are even a couple of differences between versions of the Prayer as it appears in Matthew, (the version of the Lord's Prayer most often quoted), and in Luke. Luke, though still petitionary, gives us a more present, a more "now" interpretation. He says, "Thy will be done, as in heaven, so in earth." And he says, "Forgive us our sins (not debts or trespasses but where we have fallen short) for we also forgive everyone that is indebted to us." This interpretation implies that we have already forgiven, not that we will in the future.

It all depends on how you interprete it. If the Lord's Prayer is seen as an acknowledgement of God's presence, it can make all the difference. When I was at my lowest one day, and needed to pray, I heard an interpretation similar to the one when I saw God as "process," only this time God was conceived of as the divine plan. It went:

> Our divine plan which art in perfect truth. Wholly is thy expression. Thy rulership is present, thy will is done at the spiritual level as well as at the material. Thou fulfill our daily need. Thou has forgiven us when we violate the divine plan and we release others when they are out of line with the plan. Lead us not into the temptation to doubt the divine plan and deliver us from being apart from it. For the divine plan is the spiritual kingdom, the one power, and the glory for all men.

It's a matter of intent and intent is attitude.

Prayer as Communication

I've just been ranting and raving about what prayer isn't or shouldn't be so now I'd like to explain what it is. It's communication with the Divine. It's our attempt to open a divine intercourse between our particle self and our wave self.

The first step toward prayer involves taking stock of the situation we are in to begin with. Prayer or meditation means many things: it means turning inward, contemplating reality, reflecting on the truth of being, being an observer of our stream of consciousness, our feelings, our visions and our multi-dimensional nature. It means becoming aware of our oneness with God.

If, however, this feeling of oneness remains only on the level of emotions, it will lead to sentimentality, self-negation, and a rejection of responsibility. Prayer should not be an escape from the world, but a means of looking more profoundly into it, free of limited concepts.

People who claim to meditate with no thought or to go beyond human awareness are kidding themselves. They may float in a daydream but that is not prayer. True prayer is constantly conscious. It isn't a matter of stopping consciousness but rather in directing it, directing it toward love.

In fact, prayer is our attempt to make love with life. It's our courtship. Our wooing spirit. It's not something we do. It's something we experience in union with our love self. It's a divine conversation we have with God.

The word "conversation" comes from the Latin meaning "intercourse." The same root gives us the word "converse" which the dictionary says is the Latin for "to dwell, to keep company with." So our prayers are our desire to keep company or to dwell with God. That has nothing to do with trying to make God our servant.

The desire to pray should be like the desire to be with your beloved mother or loved one. You don't want anything from either of them. You just want to "communion," (i.e., communicate) with them, and be in their presence, be one with them.

When you realize that prayer is a communication experience, something you experience rather than something you "think" or "say," you can get rid of the superstition involved with all the techniques for prayer that various teachings offer. No one knows a sure way to pray anyway. We know techniques, but God contact is something that happens "to" us. It's not something we "do."

What we ordinarily call meditation is usually some technique we have found which has helped us to arrive at the experience of communicating with God. In the true sense of the word, meditation is not the technique but the result of the technique.

Earlier in this book, I pointed out the Yoga acknowledgment that there are different approaches for attaining God contact depending on different personalities. As each of us is different, we need to find the technique that best suits our own unique consciousness. No two of us are exactly alike. There are no "best" ways.

The goal for all techniques of prayer is to bring you into the spirit of communication with your own new mind. Once the contact has been made, once one has prayed aright, miracles follow. It cannot be otherwise. "Ye shall know them by their fruits."

Remember, the first law of spiritual nature is that all appearances are the result of our own consciousness, our own attitudes. I promise you, if you have altered consciousness from a belief in "this world" into an awareness of "my kingdom," you have prayed and the outer picture will change. As a matter of fact, if the outer picture does change, you have prayed whether you know it or not.

Our attitudes are our prayers. The word "attitude" comes from the Latin word meaning "to fasten to or join." As such, our attitudes are bridges from our spirit level to the physical. Our attitudes are written all over our faces and in our body language. The minute you see people with whom you are close, you are aware of what attitude they are communicating. That means you are aware of the quality of their prayers at the moment.

You see, we think of prayers as what helps to form our outer world. Well, our attitudes reflect what we are imaging at any given moment and, as our images are constantly creating our world, our attitudes become our prayers. "Pray without ceasing," should have read, "Monitor your attitudes without ceasing."

Mainly prayer is our attempt to get our lower mind (personal sense) to communicate with our new mind (God). All the multi-dimensional aspects of our being which we discussed earlier come in to play. When we know the difference between the psychological approach (which is indeed like programming a computer with right thoughts, right mental prayers), and the spiritual experience (which is like turning the computer on), we can see that prayer expresses itself differently at each level of identity. Prayer is a total experience involving all levels. Just as there are different laws for each dimension, there are different ways to pray depending on where, when, and why we are at any given moment.

The Ways of Prayer

"Where your treasure is, there will be your heart, also." Your most effective prayer centers around where your treasure is. If you are a musician, then music is your best prayer technique. Through music, you communicate with your source. If you are a visual artist, you pray with your eyes and communicate with your art.

I have a close friend who is an artist and architect. When he needs to pray, when his attitude is dis-eased, he gets on a bicycle and pedals through a district of old houses, letting his eyes appreciate and unify his spirit until he feels at ease.

If you were to tell the average bridge players that they like playing bridge because it is a form of prayer, they would think you were off your rocker, but that is what prayer is. Look at it. If, for a couple of hours, you and three others concentrate on the cards, forget your daily personal sense problems and let your ego identity off the hook, you end up feeling repaired (re-paired with God) even if you lose the game.

People love the theater for the same reason. If the playwright, director and actors create an illusion which is so real that the audience forgets their ordinary, everyday illusion for just a moment, they leave the theater exalted and healed even if the play itself is a tragedy. Why? For a few minutes, they have forgotten their sense of separation. Because their personal sense illusion is actually no more real than the one on the stage, subconsciously they realize that if mankind can create the stage illusion, he can break the world illusion as well. That's prayer.

The reason we feel good inside when we have seen an inspiring picture at an art exhibit is because that, too, is an act of prayer. Art is hopeful. It reminds us that we are Gods. If an artist can take the mundane clay of the earth and transform it, transmute it into glorified beauty, then we subconsciously realize that we potentially can, too. That's why we love artists, they show us our potential.

If you tell most people that the desire to go fishing is the desire to pray, they will think you should be locked up. But that's the truth. They go fishing, drop their hooks in the water, and sit for hours. Their lower level superficial mind is involved with the trappings of rod and reel which allows their *new mind* a chance to speak. They are meditating. They are also fasting—fasting from their daily problems.

Remember, Jesus said, "This kind goeth not out but by prayer and fasting." Prayer means to go within and contact your new mind and fast from habitual thoughts and actions. So even if the fishermen do not catch fish, they will go home healed by praying and fasting.

Actually, everything that everyone does is involved with prayer. Even football games are mass prayer meetings. For those who attend ("where two or more are gathered together") this mass concentration on the game pulls the individual out of his or her own personal sense level into the collective experience. It alters his or her spirit. Surprisingly, America's passion for attending or watching sporting events is their desire to pray.

I believe, of course, that if they were conscious of what they were doing and why they were doing it, they would not only have more consistent results but could go more directly to the source. If people were aware of their total identities, they could match their prayer to the level of their awareness at the moment. You can get to the point where you know yourself so well that you can know which vibrational level, or which attitude you are in. Once you recognize and face up to where you are, you can figure out how best to pray, and find the best way to communicate with God.

As I said earlier, when people ask me, "How do you pray?" I always answer, "Which me are you talking about?" By this time, through need, trial and error, and many past attempts and experiments, I know myself well enough to match my way of praying with my current attitude. That's part of the "double thread" approach. I don't use just one technique. I match my method with my mood.

As my treasure has always been the spiritual search, I most often sit quietly, close my eyes, and meditate in order to align my attitude with God, but at other times, I pray through art, through music, or even through cooking.

Yes, I know that may sound ridiculous, but look: the purpose of prayer is to transform thought or imagery so that the changed spirit can heal or harmoniously reform whatever dis-ease is present. Well, if I occupy my mind cooking a good meal after a busy concern-filled day, before the food is on the table I've sidetracked my mind from its woes and suddenly I am refreshed, at peace, and in tune with my inner being. Many a time I've cooked a five-course meal just for myself, not in order to eat but rather to heal my hungry spirit.

A great deal of the time these days, I am living in a sense of God's presence and an awareness of my inner new mind. When I am in contact, it would be redundant if I were to stop and pray. In fact, it might even chase away the presence if I did. Meditation can deny that the presence already is. Sure, each morning, and perhaps at times throughout the day, I tune in to feel that all is on track. If not, I go off by myself and enter my inner closet and reestablish contact, but my need to meditate, or to pray for long hours is nowhere near as necessary now as it once was.

While we are at it, long prayers can be tricky. If you pray for hours, you can't help but become mental. You have to keep forcing your mind. By and large, many short prayers which terminate when thought takes the place of feeling, are more effective.

To pray without ceasing is a matter of attitude, not practice. There are times when it is more prayerful not to pray at all than to pray. Prayer often becomes the spirit of "It isn't," whereas inaction or acceptance says, "It is."

Perhaps it would help if we look at what Jesus said about prayer. First of all, He said, "The hour cometh when ye shall neither in this mountain, nor yet in Jersualem, worship the Father," meaning that we don't have to go to any special place or church to pray. Then he said, "But when thou prayest, enter into thy closet, and when thou hast shut thy door, pray to thy Father which is in secret; and thy Father which seeth in secret shall reward thee openly." So He has told us that if we are to follow his way, we should not make a public show of our praying or advertise the fact. We should enter our own closet and shut the door to outside influences, outside participation.

By this, He explains why prayers haven't worked. The Father only rewards secret prayers. He wasn't talking about the place where you pray. There can be people all around but if you are not making a show of your praying, it is secret. He was talking about the attitude of prayer.

As for collective prayer where two or more are gathered together "in my name," a true prayer meeting is a celebration, a celebration of God's love, a grateful celebration that God is. When two or more gather together to celebrate the spirit, to rejoice in the spirit, to become the presence of the spirit, the prayer of presence takes place.

True prayer is a time of unconditional giving, not a time of taking. The celebration of God is a rejoicing that all is already well, beautiful, and Godly. When a group can meet to celebrate, not to reiterate, they are praying.

Right Prayer

Jesus said that our prayers would be answered if we prayed aright. What is right prayer? First of all, as he said, "Take no thought for your life, what ye shall eat or what ye shall drink." In other words, do not pray for things. The minute we have a person or a condition in our prayers, whether it is our own selves or others, we are at the level of effects, of things. We have dirty hands. There is only one legitimate thing to pray for and that is God. You can't pray for things, only for grace.

Right prayer is purely a matter of spirit, the spirit in which we pray. Joel Goldsmith summed it up this way, "prayer is the inner vision of harmony." This vision is attained by giving up the desire to change or to improve anyone or anything. Never seek anything or any condition in prayer. Let harmony define and reveal itself. Let your prayer be letting the "is" appear. Prayer is an awareness of that which *is* by "seeing it," not trying to make it so. To pray is to become aware of the harmony without a mental effort on your part. Prayer is the absence of desire in the recognition of *is*. Prayer is for God, not things.

Here is the secret of prayer, contemplate it: *Pray for anything you want as long as it is spiritual.* To me, the most vital prayer in the Bible, the true prayer of recognition or acceptance, is Psalm 23:

"The Lord is my shepherd" (now); "I shall not want" (because I will be supplied), "He maketh me to lie down in green pastures" (has already prepared them for me): "he leadeth me beside the still waters" (I don't have to find my way). "He restoreth my soul" (I don't have to ask): "he leadeth me in the paths of righteousness for his name's sake" (Because I am his name sake). "Yea, though I walk through the valley of the shadow of death" (through the illusion of death), "I will fear no evil" (because there is no power apart from God), "for thou art with me" (as me): "Thy rod and thy staff they comfort me" (I can totally accept). "Thou preparest a table before me in the presence of mine enemies" (It is done): "thou anointest my head with oil" (opens my new mind), "My cup runneth over" (the cup of life); "Surely goodness and mercy shall follow me all the days of my life" (will be the results of my life . . . without a doubt). "and I will dwell in the house of the Lord for ever" (I will live in the consciousness of true being eternally.)

TEN

For-Giving

To explain prayer in a chapter is like describing life with a single word. At one level, the first commandment level, prayer is an experience; at the second neighbor level, it's something you "do," through action. Humanly, our actions are our prayers. Actions are expressed attitudes. None of us is what we say, we are what we do. We are not only what is living our bodies, we are what our bodies are doing. The sooner we stop thinking of ourselves as effects and see ourselves as cause, the better.

We don't have to worry about having to find out how to pray. When we are unable to experience some inner feeling or some mental image of prayer, we can always do something which is prayer at the action level, at the level of our humanity. I'd like to show you how I discovered "action prayer," the action that is prayer.

A few years ago, I made space for a couple of weeks of long-overdue vacation. It was time for me to return to Maui for some spiritual R & R, rest and recreation and to touch base with Haleakala. When I go on a personal retreat, I always take along a couple of books and my Bible as springboards for meditation. This time I saved a new book from an author whose previous one on the subject of love had been inspirational. I wasn't expecting anything new in the book. The books we like are always those telling us what we already know, are in agreement with us. But his individual way of putting my cherished truths helped light my fire and reintroduce that wonderful sense of love's presence.

I finally arrived, found a nice place to rent on a private beach, and settled in. On the first morning, I went out on the terrace, looked out over the lapping blue water, smelled the ever-present flowers, and opened the book on the subject of love, anticipating an angelic euphoria. But, alas, no! As I read, I felt a mild annoyance at first, but then it grew into full fledged anger. Whoops! What was this all about?

The conscious me and the unconscious me were not communicating, so I put the book aside and went into meditation in order to reconcile my particle self with my wave self. I heard, "You're getting angry because this book is laying a guilt trip on you. You always get angry when someone or something tries to trick you with guilt. The book is saying you should be more loving, that love is wonderful. Love conquers all. It implies that you don't love enough, that you should be more loving, as though you are at fault for not being more loving. Under the guise of love, this book tempts you to hate yourself for not being more loving."

I asked what the answer was and "it," the voice, went on to say, "Love is not a faucet you can turn on or off at will. By an act of will, man can't be more loving any more than he can be more spiritual. Love is a quality of God. What's more, in this respect, love is not a *cause*. Love is a *result*. As a human being, you can't be more loving but you can do something that brings on the ambience of love. Love comes as a result of what you have done."

Those who say we should (or even can) start loving someone whom we don't like by an act of the mind are kidding themselves. At best, they brainwash themselves and when the chips are down, their sublimated, unresolved hate re-emerges.

By the same token, those who say we should forgive some jerk whom we know is being stupid, are just as misleading. Thinking that we can or have forgiven, by forcing ourselves to feel something which we don't, doesn't hack it. As long as we think someone needs to be forgiven, we haven't forgiven. As long as we think we "should" love someone, we aren't *in* love.

Any teaching which tells you that you should be more loving or more forgiving without telling you how to do it, is doing the hateful opposite to you.

When I realized that just having thoughts of love was not enough, I had a moment of terror. "Then what can I do? What can I do to bring real love into my life?" And it said, "You can be *for-giving*." It didn't say "forgiving." It said "for giving." You can give, give, give.

This is how it works. I don't have to brainwash myself into believing that I have to love or that I have forgiven this jerk who is abusing me. There is something I can do. I can give no matter what he does or what I feel. I can be for giving seventy times seven because I can always give no matter what anyone else does or how I actually feel. If I don't have any pennies in my pocket to give, I can always pick a flower by the roadside and give that.

In life, we are either acting or reacting. Whenever we attack, as *The Course in Miracles* states, we are reacting to personal sense, we are reacting to our own guilt. When we give, we are not reacting. We are *acting* by giving. In fact, the only true action is the act of giving, of creating. Every other so-called action is really a reaction to situations, people, and circumstances.

Every time we desire or want something, we are re-acting. We are reacting to desire. We want to take rather than to give. And—mark this—our mistakes are just that: our *mis-takes*. Look at it, every so-called mistake you have made in your life has taken place because you wanted something. Every mistake was a reaction to the first law of human nature, survival fear.

Remember, the first law of spiritual nature is that nothing in our lives is caused by any outside influence. We have brought on every mistake we have made by blindly reacting to personal sense. A smart con-man never actually tricks his victims. He lets the victims trick themselves. He dangles a golden carrot in front of them and out of desire, out of greed, out of wanting something, they fall into the net. They do it by wanting to take rather than to give.

Giving and the resultant love are not a two-way street. You cannot give and take at the same time. The stream doesn't flow in two directions at the same time. Either you are sending out,—giving,—or you are taking in,—getting. Both do not happen coherently. Absolutely, and this is another acceptable absolute: Every desire signals self-centeredness, personal sense. There's a you wanting. Every desire is the desire to take, to get. Love is never the complement of taking; it is always the complement of giving. That's why if you want to have love, you have to start giving and love will be the result, not the cause.

Oh sure, there is an enormous flow which comes back as a result of giving. It is your own giving which has multiplied and returned to you; so the receiving that is the result of giving is really the flower of love. It may appear as though the stream is flowing into you but that is an illusion. What you receive as a result of your giving actually comes out from you, not in to you.

Here again, it is not a moral issue. Those who have accumulated a great deal in their lifetimes have given a lot somewhere along the line.

I once wrote an article called, "The Capitalistic Mystic," explaining that you do not become the head of a large corporation if you haven't at least stumbled on the importance of giving. Your daughter may be a dope fiend, your wife a cleptomaniac, and your home life a mess because you haven't discovered other dimensions of spirit but in business somehow you have learned how to give or you wouldn't have received. When financial success is honest, the successful business is the flowering, like love, the result of a business which fulfilled a need.

Sometimes people wonder why their previously successful businesses are now failing. They have let the quality of their product, their giving, drop and the flower of success has withered on the vine.

This reminds me of another funny example which explains the giving principle. I had been on a long exhausting lecture tour. After having finished a full week of church-hopping talks and an eight-hour two-day weekend seminar, I had to speak at two Sunday morning services at a large church in Santa Monica, California. After my sermons, the minister took me to lunch and suggested that I accompany her for an afternoon meeting where Charles King, a well-known baritone was going to lead some singing. I demurred, feeling wrung out. She countered, "Come with me. You don't have to do anything. You won't have to talk. Just sit there." So I agreed.

We entered the meeting hall and the minster sat down on the front row, I next to her. The singer began and led up to a rousing song in order to get everyone moving. It was one of those mixtures of song and movement where we were told to pat ourselves on the shoulders and on top of our heads, while singing, "Happy am I. I'm happy, happy." Feeling foolish was bad enough, but sitting on the front row, I couldn't very well refuse to bang away with the rest; so bang I did.

The song ended with a blast. King looked down to where I was sitting and said, "Walter, come on up here and say a few words." Well, I bounded up on the stage and gave perhaps the best ten minute talk I've ever given.

The subject was the story I mentioned in the last chapter where the poor widow said she had only a couple of drops of oil in the house, but this time it was different. When the wise men said, "Pour," what they were really saying was, "Start giving," and that had profound implications. The widow's pouring got rid of the false sense of God because it got rid of the idea that God was something other than herself or outside of herself. Her own capacity to pour told her that she was not a poor victim of circumstances. There was something she could do to activate the power of her God self. She could give and in turn she would receive as a result of having given. When the wise men said, "Pour," they didn't say "Ask, beg, or pray." They said "give" because giving *is* prayer—at the personal level.

I myself was a perfect example of what can happen. I had only a drop of energy when I came into the church but after that song, embarrassed as I may have been, I was nevertheless charged up and ready to go because I had poured out my last drop of my energy and it had multiplied. God didn't do it. I did it by my own giving.

But giving isn't just material. That is the least of it. After his many instructions, Jesus finally told his disciples, "I will give unto thee the keys of the kingdom of heaven." He went on to say, "Whatsoever thou shalt bind on earth shall be bound in heaven; and, whatsoever

thou shalt loose on earth shall be loosed in heaven."
To give is to release. The paradox is that when you
release, you get back—you "re-lease," you take a new
lease on it.

Release is the secret. To desire is to bind but to
release is to give. When you release something or someone, you are for giving. Whenever you know "no man
after the flesh," you release him from judgment. You
no longer hold him in bondage to a linear dimensional
sense of identity. When you release him, you allow
his spirit to flow. You give him freedom.

We become immortal not by trying to hold on to
our selves but by letting them go, by releasing them.
Whatever we master, we do not need to hold on to.
We can always create anew because we are the source
of creation. We announce our sovereignty by releasing
everyone and everything.

When Jesus said, "If thou rememberest that thy
brother hath aught against thee . . . go thy way; first
be reconciled to thy brother and then come and offer
thy gift," He didn't necessarily mean you have to be a
hypocrite and to throw your arms around someone you
are angry with. But he meant that you do have to be
reconciled, reconciled by releasing the person from your
judgment if you want the peace of contact with God.
The only altar is the one within your own spirit and
you can't come to that harmony of spirit unless you
have forgiven. But when you release everyone in
the human scene, your spirit is no longer bound on
Earth and you can be free in Heaven—by being forgiving.

People are the least of it. You'd be suprised at all
the things you have to forgive. You have to forgive
everything. You have to forgive life, humanity, problems, expectations, fears, regrets, yourself, your family,
the past, the process, personality, anger, even God,
love and Jesus.

You might say, "Now I know he's nuts. He's really gone too far. How can I give to God, to love or to Jesus?" Stick around and I'll explain.

After that day in Maui when the importance of giving as the action of prayer came to me, I began to get a daily message on forgiving every morning. A new aspect revealed itself each day for six months. Here are a few of them.

For-Give God

How do we give to God? Two ways: we release God by not wanting anything from Him, by asking for nothing from Him, or by even expecting anything of Him. The only way we can do this is to have faith, to realize that "it is your Father's good pleasure to give you the kingdom." Hear that? It is his pleasure to *give*. When we earn, strive for, demand, or ask for anything, then God's gift is not a gift but a payment or a bribe. But as Paul says, God's gifts come "If by grace, then is it no more of works: otherwise grace is no more grace. But if it be of works, then is it no more grace." So to give to God is to allow God to give to us by refusing to "take" responsibility personally.

First, if we don't want anything "from" God because we know that God is the only power maintaining and sustaining us, we are giving "to" God. When we recognize that we don't need to receive from God because we already have the new mind within us, we are giving devotion to God.

Second (the neighbor side), what do we have of a material nature to give to God? We have ourselves to give, our supreme gift. How? By ceasing to strive for anything, by realizing "I of my own self can do nothing," therefore "Take me, God." "I surrender my lower mind self to my higher mind self."

Third, I contemplate the circle (the bonding) and I seal the forgiving by communicating agreement. With the attitude of, "yes dear," I offer myself into acceptance of the completeness of life *now*.

For-Give Fear

Fear, "fear" communicates a fear of mis-taking, the belief that someone or something will take from us what we think we need. That's why fear is the first law of human nature, of survival.

Forgiving fear is to release the fear of being taken "from." To forgive fear is to be willing to give and to let go. If you are willing to give, you don't fear whatever is being taken from you.

Fear and things are synonymous. Take a look. You have never feared unless some "thing" was involved. When fear connects with body, it means you are accepting body as a thing, a thing with the power of good or bad. Whenever fear is connected with finance, somewhere you believe a business or investment has become a "thing" that needs protection. But there is no such thing as understanding a "thing." A thing is an effect not a cause. Cause can be understood because it is power and consciousness. What maintains and sustains the thing is *spirit*.

Whenever you feel fear, look and see what "thing" is tempting you to believe it has power, power apart from God. Ask, "Can this body separate me from God?" "Does this lack of money make God any less God?" Whenever we recognize an object as a thing, whenever we see that some material form has identified itself with fear or vice versa, some fear has identified itself with a thing—we can spot the trick. That's how we forgive fear—we recognize that we have identified an effect as a cause. Whenever we look at a fear, trace it to the thing we are fearing for or about, and then realize that things are not God, we have forgiven fear.

When Jesus said, "Destroy this temple and in three days I will raise it up," He was saying "destroy this thing and I will show you I am the spirit." He forgave fear.

For-Give the Past

Regrets, fears, and all forms of guilt are signs of not having forgiven the past. There can't be any guilt feeling without the past. Guilt results from some past action. Actually guilt is itself an illusion, a reaction. Guilt is not a cause. It has been caused by something else, some act of commission or omission. That act was undoubtedly a mistake based on desire and caused the illusory belief of a life apart from God. It is absolutely necessary to forgive the past, if one is to end the illusion of guilt.

How do we forgive the past? The same way we forgive anyone or anything—we release it, we let it go, we want nothing from the past.

Right now we must stand naked, naked of desire, naked of fear, naked of guilt, naked of trying to hang on to any person, place, or thing from the past. We have to be naked of all desires in order to be forgiving.

It is like taking a bath. We bathe daily to get rid of the past, to cleanse from the dirt which we have picked up in the process of creating our daily life. We cleanse the odor of past involvement in the market place of action. In order to return to the impersonal state of cleanliness, we take off all our memories, all our human identification. We stand naked and pray. Prayer is the action of returning to the basic pure relationship with God.

But, we don't stay soaking in the bath of spirit, we don't remain in the shower purifying indefinitely. After a while, we dry off, and put our clothes—our human identity—back on, and return from our closet into the world. We are not absolutists. We don't bath all the time but neither do we let too much time pass before returning to the purifying bath once more.

Come to think of it, the frequency of our baths to scrub off the past depends on our action. If we are involved in a dirty business, a business where we have to assume a high degree of personal sense, then we have to bathe more often. That means we turn within to meditate, to make our contact, and to release and forgive the past. When the past has been forgiven, we once more feel we are the children of God. We feel guiltless.

For-Give Expectations

The fabric of the future is made up of expectations. Expectations are like candy bars. They seem so sweet and innocent but many expectations fatten up our egos and alienate us from the present.

When we have expectations for or about another person, we create what *The Course in Miracles* calls "special relationships" and we project our guilt for having a need onto that person. We are actually attacking ourselves for losing sight of our own self-worth.

Of all the many causes of disease, expectations are the most subtle temptation because they seem so innocuous. Good is much harder to get rid of than bad. Bad is an obvious villain but good seems like a welcome friend. However, we can't, as the song says, have one without the other. They are Siamese twins. Get rid of both or neither.

The reason expectations are subtle is because they are fueled by hope and without hope humankind has a hard time continuing. Even the Bible says "Faith is the substance of things hoped for."

The catch is that there's a world of difference between "spiritual" expectation and "material" hope. Spiritual expectation is based on the belief that God is experience-able now but human hope is based on material survival. So hope is the energy behind expectations and when we forgive expectations they are no longer material but Godly. If we are to forgive the future, which is to let go of expectations, we have to recognize the presence of God now.

It is harder to forgive the future than the past because whenever we think we have the power to do something of ourselves, to create or improve the conditions of our life, we are planning and plans are expectations. Fear enters again, fear that our expectations may not be fulfilled.

To forgive the future is to love the now, to release all expectations or hope for anything other than present atonement.

For-Give Process

Forgiving means to trust in the process. That means to trust the invisible God, of which we are a part. Process is invisible though its results become visible forms. We don't actually see the process with our eyes any more than we see electricity. We see the light resulting from the process of electricity but not the electricity.

To trust the invisible process and to let it go from our desire to control is to go beyond and to release appearances. Only when we transcend appearances are we able to see God everywhere present, the true atonement. Those who walk in the light are those who love because their presence demonstrates the invisible nature of the electricity of God.

I once got a letter from Shirley MacLaine who said it beautifully. She wrote, "Those souls who walk in the light should take the responsibility of seeing to it that they express (give) the very best within their nature, the highest order of their understanding, so that they can begin to look beyond the appearance of things and see the infinite nature of God everywhere present."

Psychology accepts the visible as real and believes that man controls the process or at least can manipulate it. Spiritual man forgives the process—he lets it happen without personally trying to direct it.

For-Give Personality

Just as forgiveness is complete when there is nothing to forgive, when no thing is seen as having power, forgiveness is complete when there is no personality left but God, the only perceived being.

As long as I have an enemy, or believe that people can be good or bad, I need to forgive. When I arrive at the point of realizing that the other person's true identity is the Christ, then there is no longer any one, any personality, to forgive. I certainly don't have to forgive the Christ.

When I realize that God is my consciousness and therefore also the consciousness of all other persons, there is nothing left but the divine plan. When I realize that personal sense is an illusion, I have forgiven personality.

For-Give Family

This one is a lulu. Because the family has been the basic self-preservation unit since time began, family relationships are based on the first law of human nature—survival fear. I doubt that there is any one of us who does not recognize all kinds of tinder box emotions surrounding family relationships. That's because we have been taught to make family into "special" relationships.

We expect traditional responses from the members of our family such as the recognition of birthdays, gifts at Christmas, and family dinners. Along with that, each different relationship implies certain special requirements. A mother is supposed to do certain things, to fulfill particular needs. A father is looked on specially to be our conscience, to provide and to protect. Children are supposed to repay their parents. Brothers and sisters have special responsibilities. And above that, the family as a whole is supposed to take care of the elderly so that they, in turn, will be taken care of when they are old. In other words, we are conditioned to perpetuate the system and the system isn't spiritual. It is based on self-protection, fear and need. As with any special relationship, we project our guilt for having the need on to other members of the family, and as long as we do that, we need to forgive our family.

So how do we forgive the family? Remember what Jesus said, "Our father which art in heaven," not "specialized" as a person on earth. He also said, "Who is my mother? and who are my brethren?", and went on to add, not the physical beings on earth but those of his spiritual household. So we forgive our family when we release them from "special" labels and see them all equally as God being, when we want nothing from them. When we release ourselves from the usual conditioned response to members of our family, we have forgiven them, we have given them freedom from our needs.

In other words, we heal them. As long as we see them as merely physical beings, we are not seeing them as God beings. This is when we must practice instant obedience to the truth and catch ourselves. When the word "duty" appears, we must remember our only duty is to God, the purity of our own selves. The reason so much emotion rises in family matters is because there is so much guilt connected to duty. Trying to comply with duty, which implies God is not on the scene, leads to guilt.

We do have a responsibility, that is true, but it is not the responsibility to mother, father, sister, or brother. It is to our fellow mankind, to the family of all mankind because all humankind is an extension of ourselves. Our response to God is expressed in forgiving and healing everyone. As we are surrounded by family, we heal it by realizing our "holy" relationship, free of the labels.

Even Paul said that it does us no good to pray for our own family because that is like praying for ourselves. Today nations face the same problem. Nations are like extended families. They too make special relationships for their citizens, separating them from the family of all mankind. So nations must now change, drop their fearful and selfish national interests, and give to the family of all.

For-Give Anger

Anger, like love, is a result, not a cause. Anger, the opposite emotion of love, has an opposite cause. If love is caused by giving, or by forgiving, then anger is caused by taking or by desiring to take. When whatever it is that is desired is withheld, the emotion of pain or anger results.

To forgive anger may take several steps. First, we begin by realizing that anger is really an unfulfilled desire that has been objectified as the other person with whom we are angry. We must realize anger always involves personal sense. It has to. One has to be angry *at* something or someone. The object upon which the anger is vented (good word—that's how you get rid of hot air, you vent it) actually represents unfulfilled desire.

In other words, desire itself *is* anger. Desire doesn't look like anger until it is objectified. When it does, that is the result—anger. This principle ranges from the tiny annoyance we feel toward our spouse for forgetting to get milk at the store to a major violation of cosmic law.

Second, we begin by realizing that we are wanting something to whatever degree we are angry. The degree of anger is in proportion to the intensity of our desire. No one can make us angry but ourselves. All anger is a reflection of our own desire.

Third, we begin by realizing that we should only trust God. The reason unfulfilled desire creates the emotion of anger is because all, absolutely all mental pain comes from guilt or self-doubt. We get angry because someone has touched our sore spot of guilt. Our guilt may come from having trusted the other person. But that doesn't make any difference. When we know trust should be of God, not of man whose breath is in his nostrils, then we won't be hurt. Our anger is basically guilt directed not really at the apparent object of our anger but really at our own selves.

Ah, that is the point. We can't afford anger because it beats on our own soul. So what is the next step? How do we impersonalize and deobjectify the hurt? When we realize that the object of our anger is a projection of our own guilt, we can release it.

For-Give Thanks

The supreme forgiving is thanksgiving. In the end, thanksgiving must be total. Jesus said that it doesn't count when we give to our family—our family is an extension of ourselves. We must give to our enemies. The same applies to thanksgiving. Thanksgiving for our blessings is relatively meaningless, even the hypocrites give thanks for their good fortune. But giving thanks for our difficulties portends true freedom. The reason is simple and obvious.

Heaven is where there is no good or bad at all, where all is the divine play of God's creating. When we are grateful for the difficult as well as for the easy, the vision of true omnipotence is present. Then, all is seen as God being, no matter how it appears.

When we can truly say "thanks" no matter what the situation is, we are announcing our confidence that Heaven is this life we live. We recognize by our thanksgiving that there is no evil as such, all is God being. Thanksgiving doesn't come one day a year but remains as a constant awareness.

To be able to truly give thanks for everything that happens, for everyone who lives on earth, for every experience there is, demonstrates that everything works together "for those who love the Lord," that every person, place, thing, or situation has its place in the divine order and that thanksgiving really means, "I love you."

For-Give Love

Ah, here we are, at the end of the road. This is what it is all about—love.

We begin releasing love by realizing that love is not a cause but a result. Love, as I pointed out, can't be turned on like a faucet because there is no love *and* us, no two, only one.

The sixty-first chapter of Isaiah reads, "The spirit of the Lord God is upon me; because the Lord hath anointed me . . . he hath sent me to bind up the brokenhearted, to proclaim liberty to the captives, and the opening of the prison to them that are bound." Perhaps it should read, "The spirit of *love* is upon me." When we have given and are then anointed, we are love in the process of being. And the way to become anointed is to give, give, give until the vibration running through our whole being is lifted up unto anointment.

Giving erases desire and releases the flow of love. True giving has no expectations of return. If one is giving in order to receive, the act is not a giving act but a desire to take. True giving is unconditional and results in unconditional love.

I gave lip service to the subject of unconditional love and tried my damndest to feel it, but when I finally saw what unconditional love really was, I was stunned because I hadn't realized it sooner. It was so simple.

Briefly, I was hurt because a lady friend was rejecting my company and someone told me I should stop loving her. When I meditated, it immediately said, "No, you should never stop loving. You should learn how to love unconditionally." I asked, "How?" and it said, "Simple, *want nothing* from her." When I did, love continued—and so did the relationship.

It is hard to put a handle on unconditional love. It sounds so unfeeling and inhuman. But when we see love in terms of special relationship, we can understand. In all special relationship, we have desires, expectations, and conditions. That is what a special relationship is, that's what makes it special.

When we can love without any expectation of return, without especially wanting anything from another, our love has no conditions—it is that simple.

When we have been hurt and disappointed in a relationship, whatever love we thought we felt was conditional love because there were conditions involved. Otherwise, hurt would not have been present.

With the spirit of the love of God upon me, I can transmute the third dimensional conditional love into fourth dimensional unconditional love. I can stop expecting or placing requirements on the loved ones and love unconditionally. Wanting nothing, I can release my loved ones to go their way free and unconditionally. I may have to reaffirm my realization that they are in God's hands and that no real harm can come to them. I may have to guard against returning to old self-interests, dependencies, or patterns, but I must keep loving unconditionally.

ELEVEN

The Spirit of Healing and the Healing Spirit

Ignorance is like an actor in a summer stock company who plays a different part each week. There's only one actor, one cause, but it takes many forms. Every discord, lack, or problem is a disease which can be healed. Every disease is just a different manifestation of the same sickness, the breakdown of bonding, of communication, between the particle and the wave, between God and humankind. Every discord we have in life, no matter what form it takes, represents a sense of separation from God. I call it a "sense" of separation because we really never are separated, we are just hypnotized into thinking so.

We don't even have to know what form the sense of separation takes. The healing principle is the same for all, but sometimes it is helpful to recognize the form in order to more quickly become aware of the cause. The "double thread" approach to healing shows two ways to arrive at a truth, at a healing. You can look at a form and see what consciousness brought it about, or you can recognize a state of consciousness and know what form will result from it. You can heal the problem, either by loving God, true identity, or by loving the neighbor manifestation. From either direction, you can see where a disconnection has taken place.

For instance, if I see a drunk lying in the gutter, I know what got him there. His lack of self-love, his ignorance of his Godly sonship addicted him to looking for a bottle to take the place of God. On the other hand, if I see apparently healthy and successful people pop pills as though their lives depended on them or gulp their drinks as though they wouldn't survive without them, I know their present state of consciousness will ultimately bring them to the gutter unless that hypnotism is transmuted.

Some may say that God is not in the human scene, and that you can't see the wave in the particle. That may be correct in the truest sense, but God does send signals into the human scene. There's no light in a dark closet, but the dark does signal that the light is absent; that signal can turn you around so that you do find where the light is coming from. In that respect, God does appear in the illusion.

There's nothing wrong with having problems or being sick but there is something very wrong in wasting any experience. Illness and failure tell us something. They tell us that somewhere we have been tricked. They can remind us that we have the power within to reverse the situation. We have the power, as I said, because of the first law of spiritual nature; we are not actually dealing with the disease but with our own reaction to it. Our life is an outpicturing of our own consciousness and we can change our lives by changing our consciousness.

When I first began my spiritual search, the subject of spiritual healing not only made me squirm but confused me. Now I see why. Whenever thought is used as a power, whenever incantations or treatments need to be voiced, whenever either the sickness or the person is being analyzed with the mind, it is a mental form of healing. Anything which involves bodily action or acting on the body is physical. The only purely spiritual form of healing involves neither body nor mind. It involves only the capacity to experience the presence of God.

The "double thread" approach doesn't put down any level at which a form of healing is manifest. In truth, there is only one healing process but it can holistically appear as a body approach, a mental approach, or a spiritual approach.

Basically, we have physical healings which are brought on via anything from herbal remedies to sophisticated chemical concoctions, from massage to the surgeon's knife, to special diets, all of which are forms of physical healing. The problem with physical healings is that they are often temporary and limited by one's knowledge of physical law.

We have the power of positive thinking, psychology and psychiatry, and the many forms of mental projection where the illness is willed away. These are the mental approach. They, too, succeed to a degree but are limited by the mind and its laws. They can work but only to a point.

Spiritual healing has nothing to do with either the medical or the mental approach. All forms of healing other than the actual experience of spirit deal with healing from the particle level, the personal sense level. Particle healings all deal with symptoms. Spiritual healing is a wave experience. It starts purely with God. Wave healing ignores symptoms and transforms consciousness.

Most of what is called spiritual healing is not. When people name, label, define, or recognize the disease as a reality, it is mental and not spiritual. A truly spiritual approach to healing deals only with the spirit. This purely spiritual approach is uniquely a Christ interpretation of healing.

I wouldn't be making a point of this except for the fact that so many who instinctively know that spiritual healing is possible don't get spiritually healed because they get involved with systems which claim to be spiritual but which still confuse effects with cause and become neither fish nor fowl.

After I discovered the Christ principle that day on Haleakala, healings, to my suprise, began to take place for those who had contacted me. But the fact that I could be an instrument for spiritual healing made me feel uncomfortable. I should have been delighted but, instead, healing requests distracted me. After meditation, I saw why. Most people were not calling me up to find the principle of spiritual healing. They just called me to get something, to get a better body or more supply. I'm not a banker or a doctor. I wasn't interested in manufacturing material effects but rather in revealing spiritual cause.

I've always felt that Jesus didn't heal people to make the world a better place. He did it to reveal a principle that could free humankind from needing to be healed. When He saw that people were not interested in why He could heal but just wanted the loaves and fish, He sadly responded, "Ye seek me, not because ye saw the miracles, but because ye did eat of the loaves, and were filled."

Jesus wasn't in the body business. He was in the spirit business. He healed in order to demonstrate the principle behind spiritual healing. He was trying to give the public fishing poles—so they could manifest their own freedom—not just to give them a fish which would soon perish.

We can rip a heart out of one body and put it in another, like taking a dead battery out of a car and putting a new one in. But if the consciousness which shortcircuited the body to begin with is not corrected and transformed, then before long the new heart will cease to function. Transplants can be valuable only if they buy time in which a transformation of consciousness can be achieved.

I'm not saying we shouldn't go to the doctor for help. If a spiritual healing isn't forthcoming, we can give time by dealing medically with the symptoms while we work on the cause which is a spiritual matter.

Also, people who call up every person in sight to pray for them when they have a sickness, this prayer list here, that healer there, this witch doctor, this psychic healer, seldom get healed. This is partly because the purpose of a spiritual healing is to reveal a principle; they wouldn't know who brought on the healing if they didn't recognize what the principle was that healed them or whom it came through. If they had first tried one, then another, at a time until they were healed, they might possibly have discovered where the light was coming from and where to find the answers in the future.

Personally, whenever I attract a disease in my own life, the first thing I do is to sit down, to drop all concern for a moment, and to make my own inner contact to the best of my ability. If that doesn't heal me, I call someone whose consciousness I feel has the healing spirit at that moment. If I am manifesting a personal problem, I am at the personal level and from that level I may not be able to break through. So I call someone who won't personalize me, someone I feel is in a state of grace. If that doesn't work, and if I have already left enough space for the miracle to happen, then I don't try to play spiritual ego games. I render unto Caesar the things that are Caesar's and call a practitioner of medical science, natural medicine preferably. After all, if in truth God is the only power, then doctors can't harm me any more than they can help me. What's important is the *spirit* with which I seek help.

Take Up Your Bed

What was Jesus up to when he said, "Take up thy bed and go unto thine house." When he saw the man to whom he made that statement, he didn't say, "You are sick because you sinned." He didn't say, "I'll heal you." Instead, he implied by his statement, "I know who you are. I know your reality. You are the perfect son of God. You *are* health. You don't need health, you already have it; so walk on."

The real significance of this story is not that Jesus healed the man. His primary purpose was to be a teacher and, through this example, He was offering a vital instruction. He didn't blame the man for being sick just as we are not blamed for our illnesses. He was offering His truth.

Mistakenly, most people read this healing example in effectual terms as though Jesus was telling the man to physically lift up a material bed and to take a physical walk on physical legs. That, of course, happened but as a result of the principle, not as its cause.

Jesus's principle is this—we are all consciousness with bodies, not bodies with consciousness. The consciousness gives rise to the body, so first examine consciousness. "What is to hinder you? Take up your bed and walk." In the first half of that statement, He was saying, "What physical thing, what effect is here to stop you? I don't see any. If you believe that effects are *cause*, you are mistaken. You are *spirit and nothing can hinder spirit*." There is no difference between spirit and form. Form is only spirit made visible.

In the second half of His statement, "Take up your bed," He obviously didn't mean for the man to physically pick up his bed frame, mattress, and springs. "Take up" meant to lift up his concept of bed. Bed is a function, a place to rest. It serves a purpose. Its significance is not material but spiritual. When we see bed as a resting place for our spirit, not as a prison for our pained bodies, we have "taken up our beds," into spiritual awareness, consciousness expressed as form.

Jesus then said, "Walk." Walking, too, is not merely a physical matter. Walking is moving through the valley, even the valley of death. Walking is how we enter the kingdom. We enter on our spiritual legs.

"Take up your bed and walk" signals "You are free *now* to enter the kingdom of Heaven on earth when you stop believing effects are causes; so lift up your consciousness and move on with me."

We cannot hold on to a partial belief in two worlds—a partial belief in the laws of matter or a partial belief in the laws of spirit. We cannot believe that one set of laws works 90% of the time and the other 10% of the time nor that the two are in competition. We can't be partial to one or the other.

The only way to keep from trying to live partially is to become aware that there is a whole different (New Testament) approach to life, a whole different way of conceiving of life which doesn't involve either/or (Old Testament). Ordinarily, the "this world" partial concept of life holds that spirit and body are two, separate. In "my kingdom," there is only one. All is spirit and what we see as bodies are simply how spirit appears. Totally.

To be *in* the world but not *of* the world is to remain in society, to respond to a name, to wear clothing, to eat food, and to appear completely ordinary to the world view but not really to be *of* it—not of its belief in either spiritual power over human conditions or in human material laws which have power to inhibit spiritual well-being.

When we use the terms "spiritual laws" and "material laws," we are just finding another way of calling things "good" or "bad." When we believe in spiritual healing which converts sick bodies into well ones, we are only creating a subtle form of human good and bad. Once more we have bitten the apple of good and evil.

By the same token, if we feel people are deprived of spiritual help because they have consumed a certain beverage, swallowed a pill, smoked marijuana, or performed an illicite sex act, we are doing the same thing, being fooled by good and bad. None of that is spiritual.

When we watch TV soap operas and see terrible things happening, we don't start shouting at the actors on the screen, we don't call the police, nor (I hope) do we start praying for the actors in the soap opera or start sending them "the light." We are aware of what is taking place in the soap opera but we don't give the illusion our energy. Why can't we do the same with the drama around us? Neither our daily experience nor the one we see on TV has more reality than the other. To be in the world and not of it means to be able to watch our twenty-four-hour soap opera and not to believe in good and evil, two powers, not to think some happenings are spiritual and some material. This is also the secret of spiritual healing.

Simply, "health" is "wholeness." In Latin, those two words are the same, mean the same. When we eliminate any thing that divides up wholeness, health is all that is left.

All is spirit, all is consciousness, all is whole, one. In the beginning is the Word and the Word is made flesh but it doesn't stop being the Word. It is still spirit.

One divided in half becomes two, two becomes four, on into infinity. We can always reverse the process and reduce until we have only two, the flesh and the spirit—psychology and spirit if you will—and then we can realize, "Why, what I thought was duality is polarity, the polarity of one, and that one is God, perfect."

The minute we believe that we have to activate a spiritual power which will heal a physical ill, we have entered the soap opera of duality and spiritual healing is impossible. Why? Because there is no division between spirit and matter. I repeat, all is spirit, all is consciousness, all is whole, one. In the beginning is the Word and the Word is made flesh but it doesn't stop being the Word.

One is whole and whole is health. That is the process of spiritual healing and it has nothing to do with trying to make a spiritual power heal a material ill. Healing is the experience of oneness.

Physician, Heal Thyself

One night, I got a call from a woman in California, whom I'd never even met, who used to call me once a year or so just to make contact. Halfway through our conversation, she mentioned in passing that she was in her eighties and had been in constant pain for three years. She told me that she hadn't been out of her apartment nor had she put on street clothes for over a year. She wasn't saying, "poor me," nor even consciously asking for help. Anyway, we finished our conversation and hung up.

The next morning I, as is my custom, sat down to meditate. I always start my meditation with the thought, "Work with what is at hand." What was at hand in my mind that morning was my conversation with the lady and her statement of having been in pain for three years. The meaning of "Take up your bed and walk" came into my meditation. So I went to my computer, wrote my thoughts, and sent the lady a copy. Well, as I always say, don't put anything into print that you are not prepared to prove: two days later I was put to the test.

A friend of mine who is a homeopathic doctor came out to my ranch for a visit with some friends. I became fascinated with the principles of homeopathy as my friend explained them. Though homeopaths give what looks like a pill to swallow, there is nothing organic in their remedies. As you may know, the principle was discovered years ago that the body's natural ability to heal itself is all important and that sometimes a "bit of the hair of the dog that bit you" would trigger the body into healing itself. The spirit of homeopathy is not the belief that there is cause in effect but rather that effect could help lead to and revitalize natural cause, much as psychology can help lead one to a natural spiritual experience even though it, in itself, is not a spiritual activity as such.

Well anyway, after we toured my ranch, we all decided to go on a horseback ride down into one of the canyons. There were nine of us. Halfway down the canyon on a narrow path, one of the girls' horses started acting up. I got macho and suggested that she change with me. I helped her down and on to my horse. Then foolishly, for I had not taken time to quiet the horse and to tune in to his fears, I jumped up onto the saddle. The horse reared up, lost his footing, and came straight back on top of me. There I was smashed flat by the side of the path under several thousand pounds of horse.

I knew right away that something was wrong not only because the pain was intense but because I couldn't move. I later found out that the horse had broken my pelvic bone on both sides, along with several ribs. I also had a few other minor concussions. At any rate, one of the girls on the ride carried around a remedy called "rescue remedy" for emergencies, so she gave me some of that and they called for the ambulance.

The ambulance attendants came down into the canyon with a stretcher and I was soon whisked into San Antonio to a hospital emergency room where I was X-rayed and the damage was appraised. Finally, I was taken to my room where the bone specialist prognosticated. He told me I would be in the hospital for a week, in a hospital bed for a month, in a wheel chair for another month, and a walker for a month after that, and then I'd have to learn how to walk again.

The point of the story is that I went through the whole experience without any pain killers, no drugs, or sleeping pills. The only swallowable was that homeopathic remedy, which I understand was derived from some kind of flower.

The reason I managed without the drugs wasn't so esoteric. I realized that if I didn't move, I didn't hurt, so I practiced my years of meditation and sort of removed myself from my body, hovering over it.

After three days, I insisted on being allowed to return home. The doctor agreed but stipulated, "If you can stand the pain of getting in the wheel chair, in two or three weeks I want you to return for more X-rays. We may still have to put you in traction." I agreed.

Once ambulanced back home where they had a hospital bed moved in for me, a natural health doctor came to visit. He suggested that I immediately get Rolfed. I'd never been Rolfed before and had always queried the heavy-duty psychological implications others had attributed to this form of deep massage or muscle work. But it stood to reason to me that after breaking bones, one's muscles would tend to pull the bones together much as the strings of a broken violin would pull the ends together. It seemed logical that if the muscles are stretched, the bones can more easily go back in place. So I agreed.

As the Rolfer worked a while, I heard several clicking sounds and asked, "Is that what I think it is?" He responded, "Yes, that's your ribs going back into place." Within a day, I had my ranch family carry me to the pool for swimming and sauna.

The point of this story is that in two weeks, I walked into the doctor's office alone—completely unaided. After recovering from his surprise, the doctor took some more X-rays; so we had the "before" and the "after." The "after" picture showed the pelvic bones almost completely back in place but we couldn't even see where the ribs had broken despite the fact that the "before" shots showed them looking like broken pencils.

I got smug and asked the doctor why we couldn't see where the ribs were broken and he answered, "Sometimes we X-ray you from a different direction and it doesn't show." Enough said.

Now, the point of this whole story: if I have any ego over this remarkable recovery, it is in my joy of remembering that through the whole experience I had no feeling at all of either good or bad. Lying by the canyon path, my only thought was, "Well, this is interesting. I wonder what it all means or what I will learn from it."

My healing was a combination of good mental attitude, good physical therapy, good support from those around me, and good spiritual contact. And as they are the same thing seen from different *dimensions,* I am not going to say that healing came about by any one way nor that any one way was more important than the others. The most important thing was the spirit behind each approach.

By the way, the day after I got back from the hospital, there was a letter waiting for me from the lady in California thanking me for my letter. She wrote that she had put on clothes for the first time in a year and had someone drive her to a furniture store because she needed a new chair. She had gotten in and out of a dozen chairs, testing them until she found the one she wanted, returned home, and, as she wrote, "All with no pain." As recently as this past year, I heard from her that she has qualified for a driver's license and carries heavy sacks of groceries home each day—all with no return of pain.

Creative Pain—Friendly Pain

What is the purpose of pain? What is pain? On the surface, it is a form of intense discomfort, a disease, an annoyance, a misfortune, one that we most often associate with physical suffering. If we believe God is the only cause, we'd have to blame pain on God. And, of course, if we look at pain as a bad thing, as opposed to a good one, then we'd have to blame God. If, on the other hand, we can find a creative purpose for pain, it may not take away the pain but that knowledge can help us more easily make use of it.

I'm not saying that we are again at the level of good and bad when we find pain's purpose. For centuries, that rationale led to the theological mistake of making a virtue out of pain. Pain is neither good nor bad. It just is.

What is pain really? Pain, like an itch, is a *signal*. It says there is something which has caused it which has to be dealt with. Pain itself is not the cause. It is a result which signals a cause. All too often, modern medical practice narcotizes the pain instead of getting at the cause. When that happens, the gift which the process of life is giving us is lost.

When I call pain "the process's gift," I am repeating that life or God is a process, a divine process, which operates at many simultaneous levels. When the process needs some attention, when something is out of place, it sends pain as a signal telling us to deal with the problem. We are the losers, if we obliterate the pain before letting it lead us to the cause.

The gift of pain signals us to be aware of some misstep we have taken, some hidden cause that should be dealt with. That is why I claim that pain can be creative, that pain, properly understood, is a friend. Until we face a problem, we cannot deal with it. Ignoring the problem is a sin (falling short of the mark). We should deal with it "lest a worse thing come" upon us.

At one time or another, we all have pain. Because pain does not exist at some spiritual level and because they don't want to give pain power over them, some people say, "There is no pain." If someone tells you that, kick him in the shins. Pain does exist at the mental and physical level. It has a purpose and we shouldn't cheat ourselves out of it.

That's why Norman Cousins, in his book on attitudinal healing, advised, "Don't back away from the problem," and Carl Jung said, "Deal with the shadow side," and Joel Goldsmith said, "Know the nature of error."

"Waste not, want not" involves all the dimensions of our experience. As I keep saying, "Work with what's at hand"—whatever is at hand, including pain. If it is there, use it. Don't be used by it. We were created to have dominion, even dominion over pain. Use it and it will leave, I promise you. Don't look to anyone else. It's your pain. See what it has for you.

Now when I talk of pain, I am still being holistic. Basically we have physical pain, the easiest to spot but not necessarily the most alarming. We have mental pain and that anguish is often more devastating than mere body pain. We can stand beside our physical bodies and observe our physical pain but it is more difficult to get beyond the minds we think with and see them objectively. We also have spiritual pain, the classic low point of the dark night of the soul. Each of these pains is present as a signal, each can show us the way to freedom. First the pain must be acknowleged and then it can be dealt with.

When Cousins said we should acknowledge the problem, he added an *"and"*—"and then have self-confidence." Self-confidence destroys fear, self-confidence establishes that you have that within you which cannot only look at the problem but cure it—and then the pain, having served its purpose, will go away.

Jung said that after bringing the shadows out into the light, the darkness would be dispelled. So very often, our problems are fictitious: lies that only exist illusionally because the truth hasn't been faced. When the lies are exposed, they disappear simply because they never really existed at all. They only borrowed their power through illusion.

When Goldsmith said, "Know the nature of error," he added, "and then know the nature of God." This was the same instruction as Cousins's, only Cousins was coming from the attitudinal or psychological level and Goldsmith from a mystical principle.

To know the nature of error is to look at the illusion, to look at the ignorance, to realize that it has no substance or power apart from the problem or confusion in our minds. To know the nature of pain is to know it as a "signal," not as a cause. After spotting the signal, you can know God. Knowing God is not only knowing perfection, completeness, and wholeness, but it is also the experience of one's own true identity *as* God and knowing that within God is the power to overcome any disease because spirit and matter are one. Spiritually speaking, to know God is the same as the psychologists' advice to have self-confidence.

As patients, we shouldn't argue with the diagnosis our physicians offer us but we should feel free to reject their verdict. It may mean that with its wonderful modern exploratory techniques, medical science reveals the problem but that we, operating from a different healing principle, can deal with cause spiritually and cure the problem, not just cover up symptoms. We do not have to accept the limited verdict given us by medical science.

The principles in all three approaches to the three kinds of pain—physical pain, mental pain, and spiritual pain—are the same. They are the same principles, each explained in the terms of its own particular dimension. And we also know that all three levels, like a trinity, affect the others. For instance, the human mind, as in the case with the pineal gland, directly affects the secretion of many glands within the body. Thought sets up a reaction in the glands. We know that fear starts the flow of harmful secretions within the body. So when we find out we have a certain "dis-ease" and begin to fear, we are adding sickness to sickness. On the other hand, if we do not fear but have confident faith, other helpful glands are activated and the initial disease is decreased rather than increased.

We know that out of a lack of self-confidence, we drive ourselves, lose weight, and eventually the body shows it. We are never out of order at one level without the other levels being affected, and pain in any one of the three is a signal that affects all three. Psychological pain eventually manifests itself physically and even spiritually if left hidden.

Ah, here's the "double thread" again. You can work with what you have at hand. You can use the physical to signal the spiritual. You can ask what way is best for you *at the moment* and you don't need to condemn any other way.

To love the pain, which is the neighbor level, is to have the courage to bring it out and look at it squarely without judging by appearances. "Know ye no man after the flesh." "Judge righteous judgment." That doesn't mean to ignore the pain but rather to look right at it, not anyone else's, just your own, whether it is physical pain, mental pain, or spiritual pain. Look at it impersonally. Look at it without any judgment of good or bad, just that it is. Ask it what it is really telling you. And then, simultaneously, know that God is on the field, that all things are possible to God, and that God is the nature of your own true being.

I promise you that when that has really been accomplished, the pain will have served its purpose and will leave because it only came as a signal to begin with, and you will have embraced your pain, and have been rewarded with a creative experience.

The Healing Spirit

At last, here it is, the secret of secrets. Please pull out all stops and listen with every ounce of your being because I'm convinced that the following few words can turn you into healers and transform your lives.

Spiritual healing is so simple that it is literally mind-blowing. It's hard to believe that anything so simple could be so powerful and effective. That's why we insist on making it mysterious, complicated, and esoteric. We can't believe there isn't more to it.

To begin with, when we turn to spiritual healing, we want a "spiritual" healing for a "material" problem. The fact that we believe it is a problem, reveals the spirit with which we view the situation. The spirit that believes there is a problem is one of confusion and fear. If not, we wouldn't be thinking of it as a problem. To effect a spiritual solution means we have to alter the "spirit" of the situation—not to attempt to manipulate the material fact as such. When our goal is to change a material problem, our spirit remains at the level of the problem and spiritually you *cannot heal a problem at the level of the problem.*

We may be able to effect a medical healing at the level of a medical problem. That's fine. It's because medical solutions belong to the family of physical laws, "Render . . . unto Caesar the things which are Caesar's." If we are not prepared to nor able to alter our spirits, we had best deal with the problem at its own level. But if our desire is to find a spiritual solution, we have to accept the fact that spiritual healing only takes place at the level of spirit. Our prime goal then is to *alter the spirit* by lifting our own spirits. We don't change the problem. We change the spirit. It's that simple.

In other words, when you are met with the spirit of fear, your job, if you are a spiritual therapist, is to transform the spirit of the situation.

How? First, you have to immediately lift, protect, and anchor your own spirit. "I, if I be lifted up from the earth, will draw all men unto me." That's your first and most important priority. If your own spirit isn't free, you can't free another.

When someone calls and asks for help, it is best for you to get off the phone as soon as possible. I personally let the fearful one tell me the problem once, just once. That's for two reasons: 1. so that they can begin to release it themselves, and 2. because I don't want to anchor it in my own belief.

I must begin to heal myself as soon as possible and put some distance between myself and the fear. That means I must clinically disinfect my own spirit. There's nothing occult about that. There are no complicated formulas. The sooner I let go of the fear that has been presented to me, the sooner I can lighten or enlighten my spirit and the problem becomes enlightened, too.

I may sit in meditation until all sense of separation (the primal fear) is dissolved and I feel the spirit of oneness. I may walk in the woods until nature has revealed an eternal harmony. Whatever I do, the goal is not to change a problem nor to help a person. It is to wash the spirit, in love, harmony, completeness, union, peace, and joy.

Love, harmony, completeness, union, peace, and joy are all those things my mind tells me I should feel *after* the healing has taken place, not before. It doesn't make sense to say that if I can feel joy in the face of disease, I can spiritually heal it. But that is how it works because the Word is made flesh. The spirit of what we image constitutes the quality of what appears.

Remember, spiritual therapists are not in competition with a medical or mental therapists. For that matter, they are all dealing with the same principle, only from different directions. Psychologists know that their patients' problems are mostly self-imaged. The pathetic wife who stays with an abusive husband doesn't image alternatives and is choosing the form her life is taking. Psychological therapists can use the mind to alter the spirit and, if they realize that their goal is not to heal an appearance but rather to transform the spirit, their own spirit is spiritual.

That's half of it—the most important half and the only half the practitioner must be concerned with at that point. However, the other half is that if the persons with the problem are open and receptive, a kind of spiritual ascension and physical resurrection takes place more quickly.

This is also why it is paramount that those needing help reach out and ask for help. By doing so, they are making it possible for the therapist's or healer's spirit to help. It is necessary because by reaching out, the patients bond with the practitioners. When they express the spirit of trust, the problem can be healed. The spirit of healing is present. Asking for help opens a door that may otherwise remain locked.

In a way, the people who receive healings from Jesus actually heal themselves. They recognize the Christ of Jesus, reach out to it, and heal themselves by bonding with him. That is why he said, "Thy faith hath made thee whole."

The truth of the matter is that we never heal anyone else. We heal ourselves of the belief that there are others that need healing. That is why if there is any chance that our spirit will be affected by a call for help, we must disconnect from the problem as soon as possible in order to anchor our own spirits at a level beyond the problem. Then, after being secure and free from reaction, we should be strong enough in spirit to reconnect without being pulled down.

Once our spirits are pure, we can deal with the mental and physical levels. But if we do start to get caught up with their problems, if we can't laugh at it any more, we must keep our own spirits free at all costs or we are stabbing those who have reached out to us for spiritual help in their spiritual backs.

One more bit of advice for the spiritual approach. Spirit operates beyond time. If thoughts are of how quickly a healing must take place or what the results should be, then the practitioner is still at the level of the problem and not working in spirit. Once spiritual contact has been made and release has taken place, that contact will continue to do its "thing." Its "thing" is not to heal a problem but to release the spirit in others. When the yeast of spirit rises, the problem will have served its purpose and will dissolve. But human time doesn't necessarily apply to God's oven. Rest assured that once the spirit has come alive, it will not stop until it is fulfilled, until love triumphs.

A tricky area, however, is involved with the emotional love we receive from friends. Their emotional love may make us feel good at an emotional level but if their spirit of concern is fearful, it might be a carrier of fear. Because we have the capacity of being multi-dimensional, we can and should offer love at all levels but (priority again) let the spirit of our love in all ways be fearless.

Actually the best way to heal a disease is to laugh at it. Laughter not only shows a light spirit but it shows that the law of evil has not been accepted.

A personal analogy just popped into my head: one we can all identify with. We should be like a mother with her child who is afraid of the dark. She has compassion for the child's fear but she doesn't join in it or add energy to it. The mother just lets the child voice his or her fear so that there is no primal fear of separation but the mother doesn't let the child dwell on fear. Her own spirit of peace becomes the light that dispels the illusion of fear because in reality it is nothingness.

Once more, the spiritual life and its healing power are very, very simple, almost too simple to be recognized.

WHEN THE SPIRIT IN WHICH YOU LIVE IS MORE IMPORTANT TO YOU THAN THE RESULTS OF YOUR LIVING, YOU ARE SPIRITUAL. WHEN THE RESULTS ARE MORE IMPORTANT THAN HOW YOU GO ABOUT GETTING THEM, YOU ARE MATERIAL.

TWELVE

The Experiential Christ

Words, words, words. I keep using noise to explain silence. We are all like onions. We peel off layer after layer of personal sense and at the center is that empty space, that no-thing-ness where the soul lives, silence. The paradox is that we need words in order to arrive at the silence but until we go beyond the words, we can't experience the silence—the thunder of silence. Silence isn't something you hear. It is something you experience. Grace is that silence.

Ah, grace! That uniquely Christian word. Grace is another of those words that can't be defined but only experienced. Actually, grace is the action of spiritual healing, the ever-present process of making whole. The process of spiritual "wholeness" is purely experiential, not mental nor logical. If the experience doesn't take place, neither does the healing.

The so-called "shift in the critical mass" is the shift from living by law to living by grace. That means the shift from living mentally to living experientially, spiritually. If you have experienced the shift, you realize that the kingdom of Heaven is not only right here, right now, but that it always has been. We just haven't experienced it. The shift has been in our vision, not in the fact. We are alive. We are life. The sky is the limit and if we let ourselves experience it, we experience the second coming of Christ.

The first coming was the moment when the Christ consciousness appeared as a single person, Jesus. That moment is like the moment that a bit of yeast was introduced to the mass of the collective human dough. Ever so slowly but ever so surely this bit of yeasted consciousness has leavened the whole loaf. The loaf of humankind has steadily risen in this earthly oven until it is now almost yeasted. When it is, we will all be the body of Christ.

Those who have believed that the second coming would be in the form of another individual are wrong. It's *us*. We are the second coming as our consciousness is Christ-ed.

We can't understand how we are the second coming until we understand the man, Jesus, who was the first coming. And we can't understand Jesus until we understand that He was an experience, not just a person, and that His presence was an experience of grace. That is what the remainder of this book attempts to demonstrate.

The reason we miss what the life of Jesus is all about is because we think He is a religion or a teaching. He isn't. He is an experience. I'd like to explain how we were tricked into missing the boat.

Those rascals who first scribed the New Testament stories of Christ and those who then translated them from the Greek into other languages did their best, it seems, to confuse us. For the first thirty to forty years, the Gospel (the "news") was passed on verbally or experientially and may have retained some of the original Christ tone but it was the influence of the logical Greek mind which finally and perhaps unfortunately caused the Bible to be written down, destroying the experiential nature of the story.

Don't forget. Jesus was an Oriental; He lived in Asia, and never set foot in Europe. One of the reasons why we Westerners often can't communicate properly with Orientals is because their language and their comprehension are more experiential than ours. We are Greek based. For many of us, feeling or experiencing takes a distant second place to thinking. We think about our experiences rather than purely experiencing them. Our words are meant to be factual or empirical, whereas many Oriental words are meant to express a state of consciousness rather than a fact, an experience rather than a thing.

When I lived in Japan, I found that whereas we are suspicious of the Orientals because we can't understand their seemingly illogical, emotional motivations, they in turn feel we are dishonest.

It's like this. We, Westerners arrive at a decision made through a combination of inputs. Part is from our family conditioning, part from our peer group influence, part from our sense of obligation, part from our practical considerations, and partly from what we really want to do. It is always a mental mixture, not a clean experiential decision reflecting what we really want or feel. Our minds make the decision. Our mental process confuses Orientals just as we, in turn, are confused by their experiential process of decision.

Well, Jesus spoke Aramaic, which was an experiential language designed to convey an experience rather than logic. He spoke in parables. As a matter of fact, His teaching itself would probably have died out except for the parables. These parables convey an experience rather than a direct logic to which the mind can anchor.

They are the equivalent of the Zen koans which were designed for the same experiential purpose, to transcend the mental in order to convey the experience or essence.

In order to begin to understand Jesus's teachings, we must realize that the original Aramaic language in which Jesus spoke was completely experiential. I know, it's hard for us to understand an experiential language because ours is not a feeling language. We may describe feelings with words but the words themselves are not experiences and, therefore, we will never completely understand what Jesus meant by using logic rather than experiencing it.

Anyway, the Bible has about as much relation to the experiential consciousness-conveying method with which Jesus communicated, as a photograph of a kiss has to the feel of your loved one's lips.

Speaking of "love," that should be one of the two most experiential words in the Christ message. Another word is "grace." Both of these words were completely sabotaged in translation. Yet, these two, as I am sure Jesus meant them, are the yeast that makes the spiritual cake rise. They are meant to convey an experience of spirit, not a mental act.

All through the Old Testament, the word "love" appears but nowhere in the Old does it come from the experience of "agape," the Greek equivelent of the Aramaic word Jesus used for love. If it had been translated as "agape" instead of having been lumped together with several totally different words which had some similarity in the Greek mind, we'd probably be going around "agape-ing" each other. Instead, we confuse desire, possession, and lust with the experience of love.

It took me a long time before I could muster any experiential personal feelings for Jesus as a person, but one day I realized that before Jesus introduced this agape kind of love, there wasn't any love concept as we know it in practice.

The world of Jesus' background was a world of dog eat dog, an eye for an eye and a tooth for a tooth: cold angry law. Just try to imagine what it would be like if our world today were just that and nothing more now. No one understood experiential love until He brought its experience to them or demonstrated it to them. Imagine! Anyway, it made me a little more able to experience Him.

It took me a lot longer to realize that grace is love expressed in action. That realization made it possible for me to feel agape for God in an experiential way. Grace separates the Christ message from all others. Although I deeply appreciate the great mass of similarities and contributions or additions that all the world's great teachings have offered, nowhere else is grace experientially presented in the Christ way. It's like the air that's beaten into the eggs that makes the cake rise. No, I should have said "souffle" instead of "cake." Souffles are lighter, more magical.

The way I know if I have had a true spiritual experience or not, is if the colors fade. Sometimes I have imagined that I have had a spiritual experience. The mind has said that I have. But the false ones soon fade, the real ones, never. The experience I had on Maui that fateful day is as vivid and clear to me today as the day it happened. The colors haven't faded a bit. I can close my eyes and experience it as though it was yesterday.

When I have a spiritual experience, I have no doubt. The problem isn't in recognizing it. The problem is that I can't necessarily have the experience whenever I want. I also know whether they are emotional experiences or spiritual ones. As most emotion is personal, it is wise to be suspicious of the emotional excesses some people confuse with spiritual experience.

I've had experiences that resulted in precognition, in heavenly music, in out-of-body travel, in all kinds of "other worldly" images, but none so real or personally rewarding as those involving the presence of Jesus. Words are personal and our best means of personally communicating is through personality; so I would like now to lay the groundwork for the experiences I have had involving my concept of Jesus. In order to do so, I have to debunk the false concept of an inhuman Jesus.

The Need for a Person

It took me many years to realize that there is a good and necessary reason for everyone to identify with a Jesus, or a Buddha, or a Moses, or a Maharshi, or a Joe Smith. There comes a time in our personal lives when we each need a personal model to follow. As multi-dimensional beings, we are often at our personal, physical sense level. At that level, the only thing we can understand is something physical. We can identify with personal suffering and physical presence. We need to see a physical Jesus.

Then there is a time when we are mainly mental. In place of a physical Jesus, we need a theology or a teaching which represents a state of consciousness rather than a body. Finally, there is a time when we have had an experience of the spiritual or fourth dimension, the new mind. After that, we don't need either a physical body or a theology, but we need the experience.

However, as long as we are on earth, we are total beings who operate from all our different dimensions at one time or another. When our mind doesn't work, we'd better have a Jesus or a Buddha and be able to see God personally or have an equivalent personal presence to turn to. Though mystics have divine God experiences, they too better have a teaching and a personal Jesus to reach out to when a dark night comes along. Actually, we have all these different selves through simultaneity. Through simultaneity, we can believe in both an impersonal and a personal God. So those of you who still have trouble with the Jesus's name, just substitute his name with any other avatar or illumined person to whom you are attracted, and follow along with my explanations, and you may be led to an experience, too.

I don't blame Jewish people for getting hot under the collar when the subject of Jesus is thrown in their faces. They've been blamed for something they didn't do to begin with. As I said in *This Double Thread*, Jesus crucified himself by chasing the money changers out of the temple. They never would have crucified him if he hadn't overturned their tables, so he did it to himself. Of course, because of that, he demonstrated the most creative act ever, the resurrection. The point is he was a person like you and me.

I get almost angry myself at the way many so-called Christians cling to their suffering bloody Jesus on the cross who died for their sins. It makes Jesus some kind of self-righteous fanatic who ought to have been put away. Fortunately, that Jesus never existed.

The first experience of a personal nature I had with Jesus didn't take place until the very night before I began to write my first book. I was at my home in Key West meditating before going to bed. The thought of Jesus came into my head and I heard, "Walter, do you want to know how to identify with Jesus?" Of course, I answered, "Yes." And it said, "All right. Can you imagine a time when the word, 'Love' wasn't included in thought? Can you imagine what it must have been like for this man, Jesus to have come into the world where no one thought about love? Can you realize how lonely He must have felt with no one to talk to, with a dozen dense disciples who didn't really know what He was about until the end of His life? Well, just the fact that a man named Jesus, the first in the history of your culture, broke through to this new level of consciousness shows that you, too, have that potential in you. Can't you appreciate Him for that?" When I zeroed in, I realized that He was a person who manifested Godliness and because He did, I can. I experienced Him as a reality. So yes, I can personally identify with Him.

Not too long after that, I was watching a TV preacher turning the word, "Jesus" into a four-syllable drawn-out moan, who said, "Ask Jeeaassuuss to come into your heart." I flicked the set off and began to wonder. "Have I asked Jesus to come into my heart, whatever that means?" So I got quiet, closed my eyes, started meditating, and said, "Jesus, come into my heart, come into my heart." The answer came, "Shut up, Walter. How can I come into your heart? I've been there all the time." I experienced a presence beyond time.

The next event of this kooky nature happened a year later. I was in New York on business and went to some Oriental art stores in search of a Japanese scroll that I wanted to give as a gift. My journey took me down to a store in Greenwich Village. I got into conversation with the proprietor, a bearded and rather ominous-looking sort, and somehow the talk turned to spiritual matters. He went into an explanation of all the departed beings who were still in consciousness and asked me, "Do you have a guide from the other side?" I answered, "Not that I know of." He said, "Would you like one?" I answered, "That would be nice," as though he was talking about a cup of tea.

At any rate, he hustled me to a basin where we washed our hands for some reason. Then he moved two chairs to face each other and we sat. He said, "Look into my eyes," and began to beam hypnotic orbs at me. I sat there thinking, "Walter, what the heck have you gotten yourself into now?" Frankly, I felt not only a bit foolish but in violation of the truths I knew. So I, with my eyes still open, began to meditate on God, the only power. Lo and behold, before long I did get an answer. Not the one either of us expected. The Christ-center within, the source itself said, "*I am* is your guide. You need no other," and I experienced complete peace and joy.

Anyway, I sat for a bit longer, not knowing quite how to end the session; so I shuddered. He shuddered. We got up and he began to tell me about his backaches. I'm not for a second putting him down. After all, I did have a wonderful experience. He was the instrument for this important experiential revelation.

Since then, I have had many Jesus experiences but I'll tell one more rather simple but significant one because it was the first time that I called on Jesus for help. I was in New York finishing up a manuscript. There was a major problem to which I couldn't find an answer. My editor told me that if I didn't redo this particular section of the book within two days, they would have to put off publication until the next season in six months. I was desperate.

I went to bed that night frustrated and angry with myself for having consumed a bit more wine at dinner than I should in order to soften my anxiety. At two in the morning, I woke. Unable to either think or go back to sleep, I walked the floor in desperation. It was bitter cold and snowing outside so I couldn't go out on the street. The hotel room I was in had that over-heated skin-cracking nose-burning dryness, common in New York. My head hurt and the thought of jumping out of my tenth story window was tempting.

Unable to meditate, unable to read, unable to think my way through, I returned to my prison bed to try to sleep again. I desperately needed a friend. As I lay in bed, I suddenly began to think of Jesus. I found myself saying, "Jesus. Jesus. Jesus," and lo and behold, off I went to sleep. Not only that, but I woke up in the morning with the whole problem solved, got to my typewriter, and had it finished before the day was out.

The Fatal Word

As for Jesus, one word almost finished Him off and His message along with Him. One word. If you remember, the emperor of Rome lured all the many different factions of the early Christian Church into a meeting at Nicaea, the Nicene Council in A.D. 325. He told them that if they would get together and codify the Church, he would make it the official Church of the entire Roman Empire. What a trick! They did. He did. And they almost killed Christianity with one word.

They authored the Nicene Creed, which is still spoken today in almost every Christian Church, and still doing its damage. It goes, "I believe in God the Father Almighty (good), Maker of heaven and earth (true) and in Jesus Christ, his *only* Son." That did it. That cut Jesus off from everyone else, made Jesus a "special relationship." And that made it impossible for most people to experience Him.

Of course, calling Him the "only" Son is completely the reverse of all Jesus Himself said. He said, "I in thou and thou in me. I in the Father and the Father in you," and "*greater* works shall ye do," Nevertheless, from that time on, Jesus was made inhuman, different from us and separate; we were excluded from sonship because He was the *only* Son. From that day on, He was no longer human. From that time on, the Church implied He was flawless. He was indeed perfect precisely because He had flaws just as you and I.

The reason this is so important for those of us who are brought up in the shadow of a false Jesus is because the image of a flawless Jesus condemns us all to guilt and makes it impossible for us to experience

Him. Under the guise of love, this concept of Jesus lays a guilt trip on the world. But if we can see Jesus as human, if we can see Him as being just like us rather than trying to see ourselves like Him, His message, His life, His example can and will lead us to freedom.

The Human Jesus

One of the problems with speaking extemporaneously is that sometimes words pop out of your mouth that you wish hadn't. I'm not out to shock anyone, but I was once speaking in a church, albeit a liberal one, when I was having trouble getting across this idea of Jesus having a human side. Suddenly, I heard myself saying, "Jesus ate food, didn't He? He drank wine, didn't He? That means He belched and sat on the pot." Oh, dear; we don't like to think of our Jesus belching or having B.O. or any of those human qualities, but if He didn't, then His example of triumphing over the human side would mean nothing to us. He would then be the *only* Son of God because all the rest of us do human things.

On the other hand, if we can identify ourselves with Him personally, the Christian message becomes a wholly different experience. Let me suggest that any of you who haven't read a "red letter" New Testament, do it. A "red letter" Bible has the words attributed to Jesus printed in red and all the rest in black. If you skip all the black interpretations and just read the red, just Jesus's words, His real person emerges.

It's fascinating to play a game, to go through the Jesus story and to translate some of the experiences into modern terms. For instance,

Love Jesus . . .

In John, it is recorded that Jesus said that if anyone thirst, He would give him living water. I can identify with loving anyone who would give me living water, and I can understand what it means to love someone who quenches my thirst. But Jesus said He wouldn't only give me a drink, he'd give me the well itself, that out of my own "belly shall flow rivers of living water."

He wasn't just giving me tangible water but the source itself. He was offering the *cause* of water and once I have the cause, my supply is endless. Once I have a faucet, I can turn it on and let it flow whenever needed. Think of that. Jesus is offering me eternal salvation, eternal supply, freedom. Well, I can certainly love anyone who does that. I don't have to put a face on the person. I certainly love that person for giving answers that lead me to my freedom.

The Cannibal . . .

In the sixth chapter of John, Jesus said that we should eat of His flesh and drink of His blood. Does that mean He was advocating cannibalism? I'll admit that we do take mental bites out of each other all the time but He obviously wasn't advocating that we eat His physical body. Remember, He was talking experiential imagery. He was saying His body was spiritual, not material, that it was cause not effect. To eat of His body is to eat of His spirit.

The story goes on to say that the multitude followed Jesus because of the miracles He had performed. They believed He could give them what they wanted, more effects. Trying to show the principle that spirit was cause, He broke open five loaves of effect—bread—and multiplied them out of spirit. Because of it, they even wanted to make Him a king. Then, He tried another way. He walked on the water. Obviously, a weighty human flesh body can't walk on water, so He pulled his Houdini stunt and revealed His causal body, spirit. It was like His hologram body, visible but not an effect.

Disappointed that they did not comprehend the principle He was trying to reveal, He went off alone but they followed Him. He tried again saying, "Don't you realize these things are the result of God, spirit, cause, not me as a man?" They asked for a sign and He referred to the Old Testament, saying when manna fell from the sky, it meant that cause—God—resulted in effects.

According to the Scripture, they still didn't see, so He said, "I, (consciousness—spirit) am the bread of life." He was showing them the experiential nature of His consciousness. He was saying, "whosoever comes into the same consciousness that I am, will never thirst." He who knows that spirit is cause will never hunger.

To keep them from getting discouraged, He said in substance, as we read in John 6:65, that God is the only teacher. Unless God, by grace, brings your consciousness to the point where you can understand what I am saying, you can't hear me. He said, "Every man who hath learned from God comes unto me, comes unto an understanding of what I am saying, that spirit is cause." For those who could hear, He then added what could sound like advocating cannibalism, "Except ye eat the flesh of the son of man, and drink his blood, ye have no life in you." Of course, this means, except you see that the spirit is the cause, you are not alive.

Jesus Takes Away Sins . . .

How can Jesus take away my sins? He's been dead for 2000 years. Jesus didn't do anything for Walter, because Walter didn't even exist in His imagination.

What are the sins He was supposed to have taken away anyway? Sins are gaps. They are the space between the flesh and the spirit. The sin is the gap between man and his Christhood, between the particle and the wave.

Every time we look at the material and forget that it is spirit, and every time we believe that there is a power other than spirit, we sin by creating a gap, or by not closing one. It happens in all kinds of tiny ways. Jesus, the man, was tempted right to the end of His life even after He was Christed.

What Jesus demonstrated was that the gap closes when the spirit is reaffirmed as cause. The key word is "Christhood." Jesus closed the gap as no one had before by bringing His Jesus, His neighbor self, and His Christ, His God self, together so that we refer to Him thereafter as Jesus Christ, one. That's how Jesus took away all mankind's sins. Because He proved that the gap can be closed, we see that we can close it too.

The Hem of His Robe . . .

"Behold, a woman who was diseased . . . came behind him, and touched the hem of his garment: for she said within herself, if I may but touch his garment, I shall be whole. But Jesus turned him about and when he saw her, he said, "Daughter, be of good comfort; thy faith hath made thee whole. And the woman was made whole from that hour." Then they brought unto him "all that were diseased; and besought him that they might only touch the hem of his garment: and as many as touched were made perfectly whole."

A garment is something we wear not only to protect ourselves but to represent our consciousness. There are many examples in the Bible of the different robes we wear representing our different states of consciousness. Our attitudes and our beliefs are our robes.

What made people whole? Jesus? No, the experience of His consciousness. He didn't "do" anything. He just was. I guess you might say that all He did was to maintain His own state of consciousness and by doing so, He healed those who recognized it and reached out to touch it—so we can be healed when we experience His consciousness.

Do you realize what that means? We may wish we had a Jesus around to heal us. Well, we do. The Christ consciousness is just as much alive today as it was two thousand years ago. It never died. We can't have infinity minus anything. So today, we can reach out, touch the edge of the same consciousness that Jesus represented, and can be healed. Our faith that this consciousness still exists will in turn put us in contact with this consciousness and we will be healed.

Touch this consciousness. Touch even the edge of it. Recognize that it clothed Jesus and can clothe you. When you sit down to meditate, think about this consciousness, contemplate it, touch it. It is here. It will save you.

If this consciousness seems too abstract at the moment, then think of Jesus's life and what it represented. You can always do that. Well, Jesus's life represented the personalization of this consciousness. Identify yourself with (become one with) Jesus. Make that contact. Touch Jesus. Touch His consciousness. See it as your own consciousness and *have faith*. For *your own faith will make you whole*.

My Brother . . .

Jesus said that God is His Father but also our Father. He said, "Your Father and mine" or "My Father and yours." We are all children of God. Then, if God is Jesus's Father and my Father, Jesus Himself must be my brother, perhaps my big or more mature brother but nonetheless my brother.

What do we know about our older brother and his place in our lives? We know that as brothers, we come from the same source. We know that we have the same spiritual genes in our consciousness. We know that we can potentially grow into the same stature as our brother, Jesus. We know that as brothers, we stand in line to inherit the same kingdom that our brother did. We can experience brotherhood.

What can we expect from our brother? Brother is faithful. Brother guides his younger brothers and sisters. Brother sets an example. Brother is there in times of need. Brother protects us from those who would harm us. Brother smiles with pride as we grow in stature. We can turn to our brother when we are tired and need assistance. We can ask our brother for advice. When our brother is not present or we cannot consciously contact him, we can imagine what our brother would do in our circumstance and receive help that way.

The brother relationship is different from any other. It is a relationship of potential equality. It is a relationship that has the tie of family support and companionship without the demands or desires of other relationships. Brother is always there for support and sharing.

As a brother, Jesus fulfilled the Scripture: "I go before you to make the crooked places straight. I will intercede for you." That means that our brother will show us the path. If we follow that path, we will make no wrong turns. Not only that, as a big brother, Jesus will intercede for us, speak for us, plead our case.

We don't need to ask our brother to enter our hearts. He's already there because we and our brother have the same heart, pump the same blood through our spiritual veins, for we are of the same Father.

The Carpenter . . .

Jesus wasn't fed by His disciples. He fed them. Jesus didn't charge for His teaching, in financial terms. Jesus was a carpenter. He made His living by the sweat of His brow like everyone else. He worked. He was in the marketplace and, what's more, He told God that

He didn't want His disciples taken out of the world, rather that He wanted them to know how to be in the marketplace, but not subject to it.

How often do you hear Jesus talked about as a carpenter? We talk about His divine thread, about Him as the Son of God. Yet He often called Himself the "Son of man," not the "Son of God," with a commercial profession as His background. He was the first "double thread" man. He was both.

How close I feel to Jesus when I realize He had to put up with the same problems as I do—not just spiritual problems, but financial and material ones as well. Can you picture Jesus measuring a piece of wood, using a saw, hammering a nail, and perhaps smashing His thumb with the hammer? How did He deal with a picky client? How much did He charge? Did He take no thought for how He would do his job on the morrow? Did He plan His work ahead to be efficient? Or, more importantly, did He get tired? Was He too patient with His assistant carpenters to the detriment of His client?

To me, it is vitally important that we concentrate on that Jesus. Actually, He answered all those questions both by His actions and by His words. If we can identify Jesus with His carpenter self, then we can turn to Him in our thoughts and find the answer to our mundane problems as well as the profound ones.

It seems the greatest secrets are small, the most precious jewels are small. If we can see Jesus merely as a carpenter who also expressed divinity as a carpenter, we too can stand with our feet on earth and our heads in Heaven.

Jesus Needs Us . . .

So many of us talk religion, sort of hoping what we say is true, but unless we have proved what we say in terms of the results in our lives and the lives of those around us, we are the blind leading the blind. That's why Jesus needs us.

Put yourself in Jesus's place. He knows His healing power works when He does it Himself, but the only way He can know if that power is transferred and imparted is if His students can do likewise. He needs His students to prove it. The only way history can record whether Jesus succeeded in establishing His truths or not, is when you and I do as He did, when you and I show forth the glory of God. Jesus needs us to validate His truth, His self. Unless we make truth work in our lives, Jesus is just fantasizing.

Jesus needs us to unite with Him in oneness in order to help us eliminate our primal fear—separation.

Touch Jesus . . .

We all need friends, those to whom we can open ourselves fully, those who won't judge us, those on our side, those we can actually touch. We need friends who will literally hold our hands. If there is such a person nearby, that's fine but what if there is none?

That's where Jesus comes in. Jesus is the embodiment of His word, just as I am the embodiment of my word. I have arms, legs, and a face, and I walk around in the flesh. But take away my consciousness, my word, and I'll no longer have a body to reflect my word. If I am an artist, my word, my art, will live on in the paintings I have left behind. Touch those paintings and you touch me.

Jesus's words in the Bible are His art. That's how the Word became flesh, literally, on the printed page. Jesus is embodied, literally, in the Bible. When a physical you touches a physical Bible, the spirit and feeling within you is touching it and the response you actually feel from the love, faith, trust, promise, companionship, and spirit in the Bible is Jesus touching you back.

The touch is personal, the presence of the physical Bible embodying Christ is personal, and the words you hear or read are personal. Jesus is where the Bible is. Being personal, this is the expression of the commandment to love the personal neighbor as yourself.

I remember well the moment I had my first conscious meditation experience, the moment when my meditation fire was actually lit. Sitting with Joel in the drawing room of that hotel suite in Detroit, and when he said, "Let's meditate," I was surprised to see that he reached over to an end-table and picked up his Bible and put it in his lap. Obviously, he didn't intend to read it. So why? The book was a bridge. It represented a material or personal object which embodied the source of spiritual truth and experience. This link crossed the dimensions in him and allowed the flow of invisible spirit to come into visible creation. After that experience, I bought myself a Bible.

To this day, when I am alone, when I need a personal friend, when I need a personal touch, I pick up my Bible. I hold it in my lap and it holds me in its "everlasting arms." I hold it and Jesus holds me.

What Would Jesus Do?

What would Jesus do if He were me—not if I were Him? Put Jesus in your shoes. See Him in terms of your situation in the modern world with all the decisions you have to make.

If you have a problem with another person, particularly someone with whom you have a close relationship, ask yourself, "Would Jesus perform in the soft gentle way I usually expect of Jesus? Would He just let a person go on doing the same thing even if it was wrong?" Obviously not. After all, He went so far as to chase His antagonists out of the temple with a whip and turn their tables over.

At another time, His own brother and mother were outside the door and He was both cold and indifferent when He said sarcastically, "Who is my mother and who are my brethren?" He added, "These which hear the word of God and do it," to show His dedication to the truth of being, to the family of all humankind, not just to the blood tie myth.

He had a sharp tongue and really cut people off if they didn't do what He wanted. When the rich man asked to follow Him, Jesus challenged him by saying, "Yea, then go give away all you have," and the rich man fell back and followed no more. He was cut off.

Look at Jesus as a man. He was passionate and His profession, His work, came first before anyone. His favorites were those who would dedicate themselves to spreading the Word, who would see Him as boss. His favorites, and He did have favorites, were those who demonstrated that they loved *Him* the most. He was a tough task master. Living around Jesus was like living under a microscope. He could read your mind. He saw everything and never let anyone off the hook. You either did what He said or you were sent away.

Jesus was not "either/or;" He was "both." Sometimes it is hard to understand but He was both personal and completely impersonal. He acknowledged individuals and their struggle, and yet He acted out of impersonal principle, always seeing the potential in the individual and refusing to accept the lie. "Take up thy bed." In this, He saw the truth of the individual, his potential, and He did not accept limitation as reality, didn't let him off the hook.

Ask yourself these questions: "Am I loving when I ignore the wrong that is being done?" "Should I just take it and close my eyes?" "Should I be afraid of hurting the other person's feelings?" "Should I keep going with faith and trust that the wrong will somehow go away?" "Am I sure I am acting out of principle and not out of personal sense myself?" Then, "What would Jesus do if He were me?"

First, He would not ignore the wrong done. He was always quick to point out wrongs. Did He attack? You bet He did. He attacked ignorance wherever and whenever He saw it. He didn't blame the individual but He did attack the wrong.

Second, Jesus didn't just close His eyes. He used them and saw the truth of a situation. That's how He demonstrated the nature of error. He saw the error and realized its nothingness, always leaving the door open for change.

Third, He was not afraid of hurting the other person's feelings. He made no compromise with principle. He knew that the person's true identity is the Christ. He knew that the mask of personal sense isn't real. So what is there to really hurt? He didn't fear hurting illusion. He demanded that the people be their true selves by refusing to accept their excuses.

Finally Jesus's Christ saw everyone as Himself. He was sure of His principle and acted impersonally even though personal sense was present.

Jesus's Love

So what would Jesus do, if He were you? He would hold up His cross, His truth, impersonally and let those who bump against it learn or leave. He would put His Father's business of illuminating truth come before any personal feelings. *But*, and this is most important, He would forgive seventy times seven. In this, He would spot the ignorance, expose it, and let us know we are welcomed in His house (His consciousness), if we would "go and sin no more." Then He warned, "Lest a worse thing come unto thee."

By saying, "Lest a worse thing come upon thee," He showed what a stern task-master He really is and showed also the proof and quality of His *love*. He refused to accept the lies of those He loved. That's what love is, the refusal to believe the illusion. That way, He lifted those He loved into Heaven.

Don't ask less of yourself. Don't love with less than Jesus's love. You can forgive seventy times seven. That means you can wipe the slate clean seventy times seven, you can release others from their temporary ignorance after each time—particularly if they go and sin no more. But if they do fall for the ignorance again, you should be more firm the next time and point out the violation in stronger terms, lest a worse thing come upon them.

There's a reason why you should not just ignore symptoms that illustrate a violation of spiritual principle. Spiritual violation is like a cancer. Each time you operate and leave bits of the cancer, it gets worse. To ignore a wrong may be to allow the death of the soul of another. Eventually, as Jesus did, you have to put your own self on the line.

Finally, you should love yourself enough to act but not react when error claims to be real. The fear of hurting another by pointing out violations of principle may be there because you yourself fear not being loved, fear being lonely, fear losing the other person. Be honest enough to take action without reacting with judgment or emotion. If you are wrong, you will more quickly learn from the experience.

It all comes back to self-love. Jesus was tough, He was unafraid, He called a spade a spade—but He loved Himself and He didn't doubt. If you can do the same, you can see yourself as Jesus and His words, "I in thou and thou in me," will be your reality.

Gethsemane

Finally, I can't give you a more poignant or helpful experience of Jesus than one that happened to me during my dark night. I was wallowing in a morass of self-pity and self-loathing when something within me began to scold me. It said, "Walter, what makes you feel you are so unique? Do you think you are the only person to have a problem? Did you ever stop to realize how Jesus suffered that night in Gethsemane? Don't be so self-centered. The Bible says Jesus was in total agony on that rock, that hard place, in Gethsemane. He must have been feeling desperately lonely and human. What do you think was going on in His mind? Place yourself there and imagine what you would be thinking, not if you were Jesus but if Jesus were you. Identify with Him as you. Ask Him as you ask yourself."

My imagination took me to Gethsemane and I heard these words:

Oh, God! What a mess I've made of it all. Father, I am afraid. It's not I who is being betrayed. I have been the one who has betrayed. I betrayed all those who believed in me.

Everything seemed so clear. I was so sure I was saying and doing what was right. How did I go wrong? Was I just fooling myself? All the time, I thought the visions I had were inner messages from you. Was it just my mind that tricked me? Was I saying what I wanted to be true without proof?

What a fool I was to call myself the Son of God! What did I want? Why did I proclaim that one must die to live without realizing what I would feel when it happened to me? What made me think I could go through this without doubt?

Oh God! How this doubt poisons me! What have I done? I stood up so proud and lofty. God, I am on my knees now. I'm scared. All the assurance, all the calm, all the peace I was so certain of, has deserted me.

I must have been wrong, for even those who saw me heal the sick have left me alone. They are all asleep. I wish I could sleep but my tears keep me from it. I am sweating blood.

How could I be so wrong? I've healed, I've lifted others, I've opened the eyes of the blind. That proves the things I have said are right. Doesn't it? I felt those truths, I heard them, I spoke them and they worked. Why have I lost faith? Please help me.

What did I do? Was it because I said, 'Blessed are the meek?' That's not wrong. Was it because I betrayed the humble by telling them they could inherit the kingdom? I always gave you the credit. I always said that you were greater than I, that any power I had came from you. When I said, "Follow me," I meant, "Follow you." Or was I fooling myself? I meant, "Follow my example." . . . Now I have failed, my example is one of fears and tears.

When I said I was your son, did I say it to convince myself? When I let people believe that and follow me, did I take on their sins as well as my own? For now, I am alone. I've let them all down.

Oh, God! Somehow I've done this to myself. I taught to resist not evil, but now I cannot help but want to resist what is coming upon me. Even my prayers are a kind of resisting. That is where I have failed. I said resist not and judge not, but I judged the priests of the temple and chased the money changers out with a whip.

Was I fooling myself? Was I asking of people what is not possible of man? When I said that you, God, were all, did I deny my own saying by feeling it was up to me to save the world?

I've done this to myself. I've failed. God, let this cup pass from me. No . . . No . . . No . . . God, without you, there is nothing. . . . Let this cup pass from me, if it be thy will, but nevertheless thy will be done.

There was a silence. Then:

God, what is this I feel? I feel something gentle, like an angel of peace. Gentle, gentle, gentle. It is settling around my shoulders. It says, "No, Jesus. You have not failed but neither have you succeeded. Because you have had no life of your own. It is all my life. Yes, those who have followed you, will go as you go, will suffer as you suffer. Those who really see you, will see me for they will see the example of your life. Though they will suffer many Gethsemanes, they will not suffer the cross because you have done it for them."

Thank you, Father. I am empty now and I am full. My tears are dried. I will wake those who have believed in your word as I have spoken it. When the soldiers come, I will know that they can have no power except it comes from you. Thank you, Father, I Am.

From that day to this, whenever I feel sorry for myself or have a problem, I go to meditate, and after a while, I hear, "Walter, you are again believing you have a life of your own." We can't have a fear or worry otherwise. So I say, "Thank you, Jesus."

THIRTEEN

When Jesus Speaks

When I started tuning in to my concept of the Jesus's consciousness, it was Heaven. On the days when that level of communication came through, the experiences were like conversations I had with Jesus. We are all connected to the one source from which all has come. All we have to do is get as quiet as possible, sense or feel the state of consciousness represented by the person who manifested that consciousness, ask what they would be saying if they were talking, and listen. I would like to share some of my talks with Jesus just as I "heard" them without editing. Here are a few. Jesus said:

"I Stand at the Door."

I stand at the door and knock but you must let me in. My words that I have given you in the Scripture are the key. You have heard them both in your mind and in your soul. You have the free will to remember the truth that has been revealed within you. Remembrance is love and love turns the key.

Remember, I said that I of my own self could do nothing. Everything is in vain unless we are partners co-creating. I need you to open the door just as you need me to enter in through the door. I have knocked. I have reached out. You can hear the sound of my knocking. Many cannot. Once you could not, but now, by grace, you hear and that means I am already alive in you.

You could not do anything except that the same Father who is within me is also within you, and yet you must prepare the way by opening the door. You open the door by trust, by faith, by the realization that I do enter and go before you to make the crooked places straight, that it is my good wishes to bring the kingdom with me, that nothing of an evil nature will come nigh those who live in the secret place of the most high, that place where I once have entered, and, by your realizing that, I am in thou and thou in me. My knock has been answered by an opened door.

I do not ask you to leave the world. I do not ask you to sit back and do nothing, want nothing, feel nothing. I just ask you to open the door and let me in. I do not ask you to judge yourself for being human, for fearing. "It is a fearful thing to be in the hands of the living God," but I ask you to let me go with you hand in hand.

Perhaps you are afraid to open the door for fear that I may not be there. That is because you still see me as something other than yourself, other than the I within you who is knocking. In this respect, if I go not away the Comforter will not come to you. Do not fear that statement. It simply means that as long as you think the door separates us, as long as you personalize me as though I am an effect, or as long as you feel that our Father has to be found outside of yourself, the Comforter within will not be recognized, will not come to your conscious awareness.

When I prayed, "our Father which art in heaven," I was reminding you that heaven is within you, that you open the door of your consciousness and let the Father in or out depending on how you see yourself.

The I that is knocking is spirit. I am spirit. To let the spirit in is to close the door to personal sense, to the world of material darkness so that the light of love can illuminate your consciousness. That is where and when I come in. I am knocking. Hear me. Turn the key of my words, these words, and open the door. Open the door a crack and the light of love pours in illuminating what you now see as darkness. The light reveals that right where the darkness of fear was, is the street of gold, the gold of spiritual freedom.

Let the false sense of me go so that I, the Comforter, will not only come unto you, but once there, I will *be* you. You will be freedom, you will be joy, you will be healing—you will be what you are, *the light of the world.*

"I Am the Door."

Dear one, I not only stand at the door, I am the door. You have been wondering around in the maze of being between the two worlds looking for an entrance into my kingdom. Your confusion and the blind alleys you have explored have depleted you, and you are now lonely and bereft.

When I say, "I am the door," I am saying that I am the door that will show you how to enter the kingdom. Don't look for a material door, an effect. Effects are facsimiles painted on a wall but not real, not what they appear to be. Look to me, to my true being, to my consciousness of love, for that is the door.

Yes, there is no other way to enter, no other door but the one consciousness which I am. I have been

234 · Homesick for Heaven

called by other names, by the name of "Buddha," or
"Shankara," or "St. Francis," but those are only the
ways of identifying my consciousness, my method, different labels on the same thing. Any other methods
rob your spirit. They rob you of the key, for the spirit
of love is the key that unlocks the door.

You are my sheep. That is why you hear my voice.
My sheep and I are one. Whenever the sound of love
is heard, you and I respond to it because that is what
I am. When that note is struck, all my sheep hear it
because that note is within them and vibrates to my
call. You could not vibrate to it if it were not already
within you.

I didn't say that a man named "Jesus," "Buddha,"
or anyone else, as a person, is the door. Those labels
identify physical form but my door is not a physical
door. It is a spiritual door which you enter just as you
would a physical one. I said, "I am the door," and
anyone who can say, "I am," is standing at that door.

When I said, "I stand at the door and knock," I
was telling you to listen to the sound of my knocking
on your consciousness. When you respond to the sound
and spirit of my call, you open your consciousness to
me and follow that invisible direction into the abundance
and peace, "I" have promised you.

When I, as Jesus, laid down my life, I was only
laying down an effect. I was showing the world that
the door is invisible, not an effect. I am spirit and I
never laid my spirit down. No, I lifted it up. Did you
hear? I said, "I" lifted it up. Not Jesus, I: the same
"I" that you have within you.

Look within your own house, your own consciousness. I, your realization of your own "I," is your door.
Enter through it. Let go of this world and follow me,
your "I."

You have looked for my kingdom to be a material
existence but my kingdom is spiritual. Enter spirit. Leave

the world of effects. Effects will follow. They will be there for you to enjoy, but my spirit leads the way.

In my kingdom, there is life and no death. Death only exists at the level of effects. No one has ever died. Leave personal identity outside, see that I am your brother, and take my hand. We enter the door together singing, "I am, I am, I am."

"They Hated Me."

Hate is the result of fear, a by-product of fear, and fear is the result of ignorance: of ignoring my presence.

When men hated me, it was because they were ignorant of who I was or what I had to give. They hated me because they feared me. Out of fear (ignorance), they ran from the very thing they wanted most, love. Their fear of not being loved pushed them away from love, from me.

When I said that I was hated by the men of this world and that they would also hate you, I wasn't judging them nor did I mean to imply that they consciously knew what they were doing. It was a kind of chemical reaction to my presence. They hated me because subconsciously they knew I was the love they feared not having. It wasn't a conscious hating but rather an automatic reaction to love which takes place whenever truth is mixed with ignorance, whenever love is ignored. At those times, either ignorance has to be transmuted into enlightenment or it turns into hate. It hates its own darkness and projects that hate on to others, on to me.

You are my child, a child of my love. The world will hate my children without even knowing why, for the same reason they hated me. They will run from the love we have to offer.

"The children of this world are in their generation wiser" means that they can live in the world without setting up the reaction we do. They live by law and are comfortable with law. We live by grace which eliminates the law and is therefore a threat to law's existence.

Anything which is threatened, fights back. Surrender would mean giving up ignorance—no longer ignoring love or God's presence as love. When I am with you, the world must either surrender or hate you. Wherever and to whatever degree ignorance is present, fear and its expression as evil or hate are there. The reaction of bumping up against love is automatic, not conscious, so "forgive them, they know not what they do." If you can't forgive the ignorance, fear has won.

Within forgiveness is the resurrection and the ascension of love. Fear can't operate in the presence of forgiveness. The way to forgive fear and its byproduct, hate, is to return to the realization that everything created has a right purpose, even fear. Otherwise, you must believe that there is a power apart from God. You can't forgive others the results of their fear unless you know the divine purpose of your own fears.

When your faith is in danger, your fear becomes my signal telling you to take my hand. When, through ignorance, the signal is misinterpreted, hate becomes the result, but when you interpret your fear as my voice calling you to truth, to the reassurance of my presence, it is love expressed. Don't ignore fear. Let it guide you home.

Fear may be the signal to take action, but only if the action can be taken fear-less-ly, not fear-fully, lest hate be the result.

Since fear isn't reasonable, don't rationalize it with thought, not even with positive thinking. Rationalizing the cause of fear keeps you at its level and encourages hate. Its only cause is a sense of separation from God or love. Know that, hear its signal, drop all thought of human cause, and experience love for "perfect love casteth out fear."

Rejoice if the world hates you as it hated me. That means you are not of the world. If your worldly existence is always harmonious, you are of this world. Our lives, mine and those of my household are hid with God in love. No matter what the world does, on the third day, you shall rise as I did. Hate, evil, the world's fear of love may destroy the body of your material existence but on the last day, I will raise it up because hate has no power and love does.

I am the way, the truth, and the life. Fear not.

"Let Me. . . ."

"Let me live your life." When you hear these words, who do you think is speaking? Do you think something outside of your own self is talking? Even when you hear, "Let Jesus live your life," do you think He is someone who lived two thousand years ago? The answer is so simple that it is hard to believe. I am the you of you—or the me of me, if you prefer.

I, the "I" within you has always lived you and will continue to do so into eternity. But the time has come when you must love yourself enough to know that the "I" that will live you is *you.*

Oh, the glory of no longer feeling that the answer, the direction, the solution is separate from yourself, something you must find or earn! The acceptance of me, yourself, is what self-love is. It is the realization that the little "i" you see in the mirror contains the big "I" that will live your life. That is, it will if you surrender to it, if you trust it.

Trust me. I am the Father that is within you, closer than breathing, nearer than hands and feet. If I had not always been here, you would more easily recognize me because I would be new, but I have always been here, living you. The only new thing would be your conscious recognition that I am your "self."

To let me live your life is to let grace live you.

Grace is God in action. God is, and grace is the flow of God's life. Grace is the divine process at work. I am that flow, and I am you so you are grace itself. You are God's Being being. As God is all there is, there is no other being.

To let me live your life is to cease all seeking apart from what comes from within you. If that comes as a desire to take action, let it happen because it is I, your "I." If you feel like resting, rest, for it is "I" telling you to rest. If you feel like reading a book, read, but remember that what you find of value from the book is your "Self" speaking to you.

When a sense of either right or wrong enters your mind, smile and forgive it, release it, because thoughts of right and wrong are all temptations to let your conditioned mind live you. Let me live your life. Let your "Self" love your "self."

I have come that I might have life and that I might have it more abundantly. Realize that I am YOU and now you will be more you, more grace-full, more apparent, a parent of your "self," father of your "self."

The freedom of realizing that I will lead you, that I will live you, is dazzling to personal sense. Personal sense can't believe it. It has spent so many years mistakenly looking outside for the Holy Grail through study, through the Bible, through teachers, through meditation that it can't believe I have always been here healing, and living you.

I am here, so hear me. I am the bread, the meat, the water, the wine. I appear as your loved ones, your profession, your activity. I am the air you breath, the love you love, the life you live. You have no other life than that which I *am*.

To be my disciple, a disciple of Jesus, is to do as I have said. I said, "Let me live your life," and I say "I in thou and thou in me," because we are the same. In "I" there is no time. I didn't just say this two thousand years ago. I say it now.

You and I, we were called to mysticism. Mysticism is the life lived in union with the one "I" within, by the "I" within, as the "I." One, one God, one life, one self, I.

You don't have to do anything but let me be you for that I am. I am that I am. I am that I am. I am that I am. I am that I am. You are that I am.

You are the light of the world and no one needs to tell the light to shine. To "let me" means to let your light shine, not "under a bushel but on a candle stick," so that the whole world can see and from your light they will see that I am their light and the whole world will be lit by your light, the light that I am.

"You Love Me"

Dear one, you have sought to love me, wanted to love me, but without realizing it, you have always loved me in every way. Whenever you have felt love at all, it has always been for me.

If you understand what it is to love me, you can love me all the more fully. I came to save the world. That is why you love me. Oh, I as Jesus didn't make up my mind to save the world. I didn't say, "I will now save the world."

No, I came to reveal a new truth, a new way, a way that would free and save those who heard me from the Hell of law. I brought hope into the world. The hope I brought is not human desire that bad things would not happen to good people. It isn't the hope that you would be protected from loneliness and fear. It is the hope of Heaven. It is a new way of being, not a changed old way.

You love me because I brought God to you. Before I came, God was something other than yourself, separate from you, something to be feared. God was an angry task master, impossible to please. But I showed you by my words and by my life that God is love and that because God is within me, God is within you and therefore you can love as I love. So every time you love, you are loving me, honoring what I brought. You are not a helpless victim of circumstances and every time you realize that, every time you know that there is a way out of the Hell of personal sense, you are loving me. That is how you love me, that is when you love me.

Feel the freedom, feel the possibility of love. Know that, because I did it, because I invented a life lived by grace, you can. That is my gift to you and you love me for it. You are free. You don't have to live by the laws of dog-eat-dog, of inevitable misery and punishment. You have seen that "this world," the world of dollars and cents, of sickness and health, of good and bad is only one plane of existence. My birth has shown you an entirely different level as well as how to attain it.

Every time you feel this presence and possibility, you are loving me. Yes, I was a man and you can love me as a man because I was a man who represented the spirit, the spirit of freedom, love, and peace. So you love me as a man for that, but you love me as the spirit because you are me both as a person and the spirit as I was, and because my spirit was love, you are loving and being one with me every time you experience love.

All you have to do is to think what the world would be like if there were no possibility of experiencing love in your life. I have not healed you in the past to prove that good is stronger than bad, that health is more desirable than sickness. If I had done that, I would have done no more than represent the same old level of good and bad. No, I heal to show you the miracle of the Word made flesh. I came to show you that you could be on earth and still enter the dimension of love and freedom I call "my kingdom."

Every time you wake from the hypnotic belief in good and bad, that bad things can happen to good people, that you are a victim of the primal fear of separation from God, you are loving me because you are demonstrating that what I showed the world has indeed saved it. I did not die in vain.

Remember, every time you feel that you are hopelessly trapped in the world, you are not loving me. Every time you flick the switch of love, turn on the light where you are, and break the dream of fear, you are loving me. That is what healing is.

In this day of material power, the only way the world will be saved is by your consciousness, by a transformation of consciousness from the world of two powers to the world of one power. You are my arms and legs. Use my love. The more you use it, the more you are loving me.

I said to the man at the pool, "Take up your bed." I said, "Deny this body and in three days I will raise it up." Spirit is up. Take up your consciousness from the world of good and bad into my spiritual dimension. You will free the world. That is the upper room, the room in your consciousness that I came to open. I am the door to that room. Come in. Come up. Believe it is so. You will be up there with me.

"Share With Me."

My dear, if you will but listen, I will share with you all that I have. Commune with me. To take communion is to share with me, but sharing is a two-way street. I will give of myself to you if you will open yourself, if you will communicate with me, and I will receive you if you share yourself with me.

The primal fear of loneliness is only the breakdown of communications between us. That is why you feel lonely. When the lines are open and our communion flows back and forth between us, there is no fear, no loneliness. So when you feel disturbance or anxiety, realize that, for some reason, our communications have temporarily been interrupted. Do not try to change anything in the without, in the world of effect, but go within and reestablish communication with me. The outside harmony will return once we are back in communication, once we are both sharing.

Listen to me and I will listen to you. It is the spirit of our sharing that is important. That is what the spiritual life is, the spirit of sharing, giving. To love God is to communicate with God and God returns that love by loving neighbor, the personal sense.

The miracle of my message is that I so loved the world of personal being that I opened communication between the world and God by my being. God communicated himself as myself to yourselves. We are one when we communicate. Love is what we communicate.

"Accept Me."

My beloved, it is more important how you accept than whether you accept. I am not a body, I am grace, I am givingness. Whether you acknowledge me or not, I am always pouring forth for you. The free flow of love between us depends on how you accept my love.

I know, it is harder to accept than to give. When you are giving, you feel close to me but when you are taking, you are frightened because your mistakes have come from mis-taking. Unless you can accept me graciously the circle is not complete and you cannot give to me either.

You are afraid to accept my miracles in your life because you may cut yourself off if you rejoice in the miracle rather than my spirit which brought it to you. That is true. "Rejoice because your names are written in Heaven." That is acceptance. If you are afraid of miracles, you are rejecting yourself but if you are blinded by the miracle, you are rejecting me.

Accept the miracle, knowing that the form it has taken is the form of grace. Accept the miracle, knowing you are accepting your oneness with me, that I am in you and you in me. Accept the miracle, do not fear it.

Miracles are God's winks. With a smile on God's face, He winks at us to let us know it is all a divine game. Winks laugh at the law. Miracles are God's humor. So, my beloved, accept them with joy and laughter. My miracles are my way of showing you that you are not subject to the laws of this world. Accept my miracles as an announcement of our secret that you are not subject to the limits of this world. If you rejoice in your freedom, the forms of the miracle have not blinded you, you have not cut yourself off.

Accept me without fear, for I am the miracle. Accept the miracle as though you are accepting me and you are accepting your own sonship in turn.

Miracles say, "You are about my business and I rejoice with you for you are my son in whom I am well pleased."

"Represent Me."

Don't you see, how can you be my representative? How can you re-present me—make me present again— if you are not a re-present-ative, a clone, a model, a replica of me? As long as my teaching and example are something that happened two thousand years ago, I cannot be present. The only way I come into the world today is through you, through being re-presented by you. You must be my presence.

My facade, my face, my visage, or my physical appearance is not me. That costume of self dissolved two thousand years ago. That was not me. "I am the way, the truth, and the life." This is what you must re-present. You must now be the way. I know that is hard to image. How can a person be a way? A person can't. I am asking you not to imitate my person but to represent what I signaled.

I am a process. I am a freedom. I am a peace the world knows not of. When you re-present the process, when you express spiritual being, you are my agent. In order to re-present me, to be my presence, you must actually be "me," not think of me, not have faith in me, not talk about me, but be me.

I am spiritual. I have used many names. I have been called by many names, but it has always been "I," the same "I" that is within you. If I were not already within you, you could not re-present me. I was Isaiah when I said in the Old Testament, "The spirit of the Lord God is upon me. Now I am ordained to open the eyes of the blind." I was Jesus when I voiced those same words once more. I wasn't either unless and until the spirit was upon me. Then I presented the healing Christ to the world, not before and not after, only when.

When you have the spirit of the Lord God upon you, you are representing me, your true self. You must be the way, not a person, a way. What way? The way of peace, of assurance, of trust, of spirit.

Now all the lessons I have been teaching you, all the trials you have been put through, are neither lessons nor trials; they are exercises calling for you to be my presence. Through them, you have demonstrated the way, grown into the way. You had to. Without doing it, without experiencing it, without illustrating it yourself, you could not attain the spirit of the Lord God and until you were in the spirit, you could not be me— be the way—for I am the way, the only way.

Go through my instructions. Look at the way I did it. When I said such things as, "Go without purse or script," I wasn't talking about money or possessions as such. I was talking about a way, a way that is dependent on spirit, not on material things, not on effects.

To be the way, you do not have to live in deprivation, sackcloth and ashes, but you do have to demonstrate a way that is not dependent on things. Appearances are things. You must be the way of the spirit which is invisible to human sense.

Remember, my way made no sense to the wise of that time and does not to the wise of today. You must come as children, children of God, trusting the invisible as children trust their parents.

As I, you do not turn your back on those who are in the world. You are here to show them *the* way. You are here to re-present me, to be my presence. You can't do it if you still fear, if you are not willing to give up your pearl of great price.

I am dependent on you to be the way today because my lessons were given to a different world than the one which is evolving today. The lessons are the same, the way is the same, but this is a more spiritual world, a world where spirit is more necessary. I cannot demonstrate the way in terms of today. My examples applied to a much more basic one-sided world. I need you to present the truth of me in terms of today. You can only do that by experiencing today's complications in the way spirit triumphs. Then you ARE the way, and I am in thou and thou in me.

I do come again. There is a second coming. Don't you realize that *you are my second coming?* When you are the way, when you are re-presenting me, then I came again.

"Share My Joy."

I sing with joy. Your training is almost over. I know it seems that you have been learning for such a long time. Every step was necessary. You have had a particular job to do, a particular expression. Now your time has come and I rejoice with and for you.

I know that you feel as though you are inferior

sometimes, that you feel you lack the faith or love that others were blessed with, but you aren't inferior. You have kept on keeping on. You have never been satisfied with separation. Now I can say, "Well done, good and faithful servant; thou hast been faithful over a few things, I will make thee ruler over many things."

You have not faked it. You haven't settled for material well-being, and I have driven you on. Something in you, my being within you, has kept you on the path. Now I will bless you with the awareness that you have longed for—"You are my son in whom I am well pleased."

Your work is over. Now we will play. The veil is lifted. The time has finally come when the purpose of your life is to be expressed in universal consciousness, this union of body, mind, and spirit.

No longer will you feel alone. I will always be holding your hand. You will not have to struggle to feel my presence. We are one.

FOURTEEN

My Prayer

I, Walter, no longer feel alone. I do not have to struggle to feel God's presence. Ever since I entered the mystical path, there has been this burning light at the top of the stairway to Heaven beckoning me, drawing me to the realization that "I am." An awareness of God within me has become a reality. I have experienced that I am the same "I am," that Jesus proclaimed when He said, "I am in thou and thou in me."

Here I stand, like the cross, a bridge between Heaven and earth. Every trial and every joy are included in my being, for every experience I have had has been a part of the divine plan embodied in the cross, this symbol of my self, my "double thread" self.

My new mind is in Heaven, my feet are on earth. I stretch my arms out. One is the positive, the other the negative. One is the masculine, the other the feminine. One is the spiritual, the other the material. One is mystical, the other the psychological. One is strong, the other is weak. They embrace my total being. Through the cross, I am both vertical and horizontal. I am both infinite and finite. I am complete through the cross. It has given me a new birth, a new self, a total self.

I want to pray. There's a part of me which isn't satisfied if I can't talk with God. Though I want to reach out, I know at the same time that God is not outside of myself, that the Father is within. That is where I can and must commune with myself, so I can become as a little child and pray to my Father which is within. I can feel His presence within me. I know that I am talking to that which is my true being. I am a total presence including God. I am my "son of man" self with its personal feelings, personal longings, personal fears, and I am my "son of God" self with its spiritual nobility. I am both.

When I lie in bed, I am not alone. We are there, and we can talk with each other. When I watch a sunset, we can communicate because I am in the sunset as we have come from the same source. When I hear a bird's song, it is my prayer. If I wish, I can pray out loud to the "me" who will listen, to the divine self that I know is my true being, and when I do, that presence will answer me back, for we are one.

I am praying to myself, to the infinite self, the wave self, the Father who is greater than I, the universal omnipotence, the ever-present reality of all being. I am praying to the I that I am.

Sometime in meditation, I hear, "This is my son in whom I am well pleased." When I do, I know a healing or a revealing has taken place, that God is truly the life of not only me but of every being and that everyone is an offspring of God in whom God is well pleased. There is no such thing as a lost soul when time is dissolved and Heaven is revealed here and now.

And when I hear, "Well done, good and faithful servant," I know I have entered the door. Now I hear,

"Welcome home. Let us kill the fatted calf. Rejoice, your name is writ in Heaven." And I offer myself this prayer:

Father, within my soul is the deep well of peace. You have gone before me to reveal that there are no crooked places. The slate is clean, for the overturning has brought me home. I am no longer homesick for Heaven for I have never left home.

I hear the still small voice telling me of the wonders all around. In the stillness, you have taught me how to forgive. I forgive the past and the future. I forgive. I release myself, my brothers and sisters, my home, my business, my sense of God. I release expectations, for all is already here in Heaven.

Father, I thought I was living my life. I thought that I had a life of my own. But I have always been living by grace and grace alone. Grace has lived me. Grace is my life and grace never ceases.

Father, I celebrate you for gratitude is the celebration of grace. I am full of grace, full of gratitude for the total self that I am. I give. I give it all to you. You are the universe. I steward your presence. I rejoice in your presence, for I am that presence.

And God speaks to me saying:

I am you as your body, I am you as your mind, I am you as your spirit. You are not limited to a finite body or a finite mind. You are the energy of the universe. See yourself flowing out as spiritual energy into the universe. This energy is peace but by being peace, it is no less your aura, no less your mind, no less your body. It is light. Yes, you are the light of the whole world.

I say to you, I, this "I" of your own being, this light has illuminated the darkness, has made you whole. You are harmony. You are the way. You are the truth. You are the life.

I have spoken through the lips of many people. I am now speaking through the lips of Walter, but it is not Walter, it is I, it is you, it is the I within you that is speaking to you.

Oh, dare to believe me. I am that I am. I am that you are. Together we are oneness. And in that oneness is everyone you know, because your oneness with me constitutes your oneness with all spiritual being and idea. The perfection that is within you is the perfection which is within them. Because there is one perfection, that one perfection I am.

Be still, be still, and love. I am all these things and I am the truth of your being. There is no other.

I hand you a little flower. It is a bud. A little rose bud within you. See the petals opening for this rose bud. See the color, smell the fragrance, hear the music, for they are I within you. And this I, this little gift, is the embodiment of love. I am embodied within you as love and as your new mind. And though this is a delicate little flower, it is all powerful because it is me expressing myself as healing, as joy, as beauty, and as fulfillment.

The kingdom of Heaven is right here, right now, not because it has come to you but because it *is* you. You are the kingdom of Heaven.

Oh, my beloved, you have looked for the Holy Grail, you have searched for the Holy Grail and all the time it has been within you because I am within you. Love me. Don't reject me by believing there are powers of evil. Come within me and let me heal. Know that I within you will heal those who reach out to you. As you walk through the earth, people will receive healing because where you go, I go. I am that presence. I am that love.

When we were young we saw through a glass darkly but now face to face. Everything you have learned so far, I have brought to you, I have given to you. Trust me and know that you are many, many infinite identities and that is why you can heal. If you are not one with your brother, you cannot heal him when he needs help because you would be two and separate, but you are one with your brother because of me. Because I am within,

I am you, and I am your brother. We are one. We are
all cells in one body. And I am that body. I am the way,
and I am the truth, and I am the life.

Fear not, it is I. Fear not, it is love. The kingdom of
Heaven is already here. It has always been but you had
to go through every stage in order to find out who you
really are, that you and I are one.

Let all sense of separation go. For this minute, the
bridegroom cometh carrying a beautiful flower, this
blossoming rose, this sweetness, this thing that goes beyond words, this deep well of silence, this peace that is
within. Rejoice because the day has come when we see
the blossoming all over the universe. It has come. Children
are born with this bud within them ready to blossom.
Fear not.

Rest, rest, rest in me. For I have never left you nor
will I ever leave you. Though you have made your bed
in hell, I have always been there. You know I have been
there.

Smile at your human self. Look down on your human
self and see it as though you are standing beside it. Love
it. Caress it. Thank it for every problem you have had
because every problem has led you to the realization that
I am you. I am really you and you are not alone. You
don't need to be homesick any longer because you are
home. Home is not a place, not an effect. Home is a
state of consciousness. Home is *me*. I am home. You
can search the whole world of appearances and not find
it, but once you look within, where the Holy Grail is,
you will find it. That Holy Grail is home and I am that
Holy Grail.

Yes, when you feel lonely, you can call on the name
of those whom I have spoken through. You can call on
Jesus, on Buddha, on Ramakrishna, on Joel, on any number of forms I have become, and I will be there. I will
speak through them if that is necessary, but realize it is
I who is speaking to you from within you, and I am
you, and we are joined together, the bridegroom and
the bride. I have bonded. What we are doing now is
bonding.

Be still. Dare to believe that this treasure is really yours for I within you have given it to you. Oh, aren't you feeling my presence? Because there is only one presence in this room.

Now we have a secret. When you return to the world, you can wink at each other, knowing that you go about your business tending to the world's problems, you can heal, you can look at patients in the hospital, but you look at them with love not with fear because you know I am that patient. Wherever I am, there is freedom, peace, joy, and no judgment.

Let us return to the world with joy because you are the window through which I shine. I am the light of the world and I need every window so that we can bring the world into the light, into the realization that Heaven is here right now.

Ah, you have told me one more thing. You are grateful and gratitude is the recognition of grace. And the recognition of grace testifies that I am the only power and the only life that is operating in your life. Thank you, my love, for your gratitude. Your gratitude is the kiss that has bonded us together into eternal oneness.

Your gratitude is the key which has opened the gate of Heaven. You are no longer homesick. You are home. You no longer have to wait. Heaven is now on Earth and we are there together. Amen.

THOSE WHO WISH to communicate with the author or receive information about recordings, lectures, and publications direct your correspondence to Walter Starcke, Guadalupe Press, P.O. Box 865, Boerne, Texas 78006